TESTING

TESTING

BEHIND THE SCENES AT CONSUMER REPORTS

1936–1986

The Editors of Consumer Reports Books with Monte Florman

Introduction by Walter Cronkite

Consumers Union, Mount Vernon, New York

Library of Congress Cataloging-In-Publication Data

Testing: behind the scenes at Consumer Reports, 1936–1986.

  1. Commercial products—Testing. 2. Consumers Union of United States.
I. Florman, Monte. II. Consumer Reports. III. Consumer Reports Books.
TX335.T434   1986   363.1′96′0973   86-70829
ISBN 0-89043-064-0
ISBN 0-89043-056-X (pbk.)

First Printing, October 1986

Design: The Sarabande Press

Photo research: Esther Brumberg

Manufactured in the United States of America

Testing is a Consumer Reports Book published by Consumers Union, the
nonprofit organization that publishes *Consumer Reports*, the monthly
magazine of test reports, product Ratings, and buying guidance.
Established in 1936, Consumers Union is chartered under the
Not-For-Profit Corporation Law of the State of New York.

   The purposes of Consumers Union, as stated in its charter, are to
provide consumers with information and counsel on consumer goods and
services, to give information on all matters relating to the expenditure of
the family income, and to initiate and to cooperate with individual and
group efforts seeking to create and maintain decent living standards.

   Consumers Union derives its income solely from the sale of *Consumer
Reports* and other publications. In addition, expenses of occasional public
service efforts may be met, in part, by nonrestrictive, noncommercial
contributions, grants, and fees. Consumers Union accepts no advertising or
product samples and is not beholden in any way to any commercial interest.
Its Ratings and reports are solely for the use of the readers of its
publications. Neither the Ratings nor the reports nor any Consumers Union
publications, including this book, may be used in advertising or for any
commercial purpose. Consumers Union will take all steps open to it to
prevent such uses of its material, its name, or the name of *Consumer
Reports*.

CONTENTS

PREFACE

To many of the millions who read *Consumer Reports* magazine, Consumers Union is known primarily as a testing organization. We have, for fifty years, subjected product claims and advertising ballyhoo to the impartial analysis of our laboratories.

Testing: Behind the Scenes at Consumer Reports, 1936–1986 celebrates the Fiftieth Anniversary of Consumers Union with a photographic tour of those laboratories. From suntan lotion to lawn sprinklers, from wringer washing machines to black-and-white television consoles, from lipstick to trash bags, *Testing* shows and tells what goes on behind the scenes when Consumers Union tests and evaluates products. Dozens of photographs from Consumers Union's archives, many of which have never before appeared in print, provide an inside look at how our engineers and technicians work.

It might seem somewhat incongruous that our testing history includes almost the same number of photos from the first ten years of CU's existence, when there was practically no budget for it, as from the most recent ten years, when millions of dollars a year are spent on testing. In the early days, CU took every possible opportunity to show what was being done in its very limited laboratories. As the laboratories became increasingly well equipped, however, photos of *how* the testing was done gave way to photos of *what* was being tested.

For this book, we chose photographs that most dramatically demonstrate the ingenuity of the CU testers, and photographs that say something interesting about CU, regardless of what is being tested. Our selection of photos, it turns out, not only documents our own history, but says something about American consumerism over the past fifty years as well.

As the marketplace has grown more complex and confusing over the last half century, CU has kept pace. And surely consumers have needed our impartial product information more and more, to help make their way through the maze. This book is a unique chronicle of a fascinating aspect of CU's effort to make the marketplace safe, sane, and fair for consumers.

Rhoda Karpatkin
Executive Director
Consumers Union

INTRODUCTION BY WALTER CRONKITE

There are those in this nation of ours who believe that some insidious process is eroding the quality of goods and services we buy. That the cars that made America a mobile society, and many of the products we use, wear out too soon and break down too often. That food seems somehow less tasty, clothing less well-made. That brand names we once trusted as beacons of quality no longer shine so brightly. That sometimes, our very health and safety are threatened.

There is the perception that in today's rush for quick and large profits, what seems to be fading from the marketplace is the quality of integrity, properly defined as "adherence to moral principle and character, uprightness, honesty."

For 50 years, Consumers Union has kept its integrity polished to a mirror's gleam, and it has prospered by stoutly adhering to those rare qualities of moral principle and character, uprightness and honesty.

The organization that began with a few people meeting in a garage, today has assets that would make Harvard's most ambitious MBAs proud: 270 highly skilled employees, well-equipped testing laboratories, and the confidence of generations of consumers.

Each month, more than 3 million loyal readers receive its core magazine, *Consumer Reports*. And many millions more "borrow" the magazine—sometimes permanently—from friends, libraries, and doctors' offices.

But its single greatest asset is that invisible, invaluable thing called integrity. The road has not been an easy one, all downhill with no twists or bumps. But it has been challenging and rewarding.

The social institution of testing products for consumers is a twentieth century invention, devised, defined, and described in the 1927 best-seller, *Your Money's Worth*, by the noted economist and writer Stuart Chase and a young engineer, Frederick J. Schlink.

In 1929, responding to a barrage of mail triggered by *Your Money's Worth*, Schlink converted a small consumers club he was operating in a garage in White Plains, New York, into a testing organization. He named it Consumers Research. In December, two months after the Great Crash, he began to publish a regular bulletin and consumer pamphlets.

Four years later, Arthur Kallet, an MIT graduate, joined Schlink to publish a second seminal work,

100 Million Guinea Pigs. Its premise: Americans had become "unwitting test animals in a gigantic experiment with poisons conducted by food, drug, and cosmetic manufacturers." Whatever the mass media thought, the masses turned it into one of the best-sellers of the decade.

Consumers Research was in business. It moved from White Plains to a small laboratory in bucolic Washington, New Jersey. Within a short time, management difficulties provoked the workers to form a union to protect their jobs. When a Consumers Research chemist was summarily fired for his efforts to gain recognition for the new union, the workers went on strike. The strike proved to be protracted, bitter, and even occasionally violent. The police moved in. Strikers were arrested and jailed.

From all this was born an entirely new organization. In February 1936, Kallet and some 30 former Consumers Research staffers created Consumers Union of United States. To this day, no one can explain with certainty why the word "the" was left out of the name. But Consumers Union of United States it was . . . and would remain.

Dewey Palmer—who held a similar position at Consumers Research—was named technical director. Colston Warne was elected president, and the board of directors included John Heasty, the fired chemist; Rose Schneiderman, president of the Women's Trade Union League; A. Philip Randolph, president of the Brotherhood of Sleeping Car Porters; and Heywood Broun, president of the Newspaper Guild. Kallet was named director.

In May 1936, *Consumers Union Reports*, as the magazine would be known for several years, ventured forth into the world. Tough-minded and sassy, it was an editorial alchemy of defiance, vision, and penury.

The magazine's purpose was "to give information and assistance on all matters relating to the expenditure of earnings and the family income; to initiate, to cooperate with, and to aid individual and group efforts of whatever nature and description seeking to create and maintain decent living standards for ultimate consumers."

Hardly a simple task. And one at which Consumers Union is still working.

Into its antique brick headquarters building in Mount Vernon, New York, flows a constant stream of appliances, tools, food, television sets, computers, and all manner of other things, and all that comes out is words. There, more attention may be paid to quality, value, and safety than at any factory in the world. At Consumers Union, high tech blends with high ingenuity. If there isn't a machine built to test a product, the testers design and build one.

In one corner, there is a rotating drum that tosses luggage about like a giant salad spinner. In another, a big green machine bashes mattresses with a derriere-shaped pommel. Rows of fancy outdoor barbecue grills, poised like space vehicles in a Stephen Spielberg movie, seem to be waiting for a call to action in the Great Hamburger Test.

The staff's favorite test site recently was the small appliance lab, where people in white coats worked turning out vanilla ice cream, which then went on to the sensory lab for taste evaluation. There testers sat in isolation booths so they couldn't see their neighbors, working in silence.

For decades, CU has been fabled for its lavish banquets for nobody—essential preludes to testing dishwashers. This unusual ritual involves laying out great tables, placing dinnerware on them, and rigorously coating each dish with the remnants of a great feast. So much gravy here, a chocolate pudding stain there—all scientifically applied according to a predetermined pattern.

In CU's chemistry lab, smears of hand lotions dry on a hundred glass plates. In the laundry room, ultraviolet light detects ingredients that whiten without cleaning. In the special projects lab, one of the more burly staffers kicks in a door, again and again, testing locks.

In the 1960s, a television commercial showed how a damp Kleenex could resist tearing when Harry James placed it like a mute over his trumpet and hit a high note. At CU, the sneezer isn't a trumpet but a machine—a wonderful wooden pendulum with holes covered by tissues. Assaulted by attacks of wind and water, their strength is measured with greater accuracy, if less harmony.

It is a factory laboratory dedicated to making sense. Its challenge to every product: Show me, prove it, perform as advertised. And throughout its history, Consumers Union has campaigned against products that could be proven unsafe.

When CU first discussed doing a report on cigarettes in 1936, it was in a smoke-filled room. Advertising hyperbole was the target, not tobacco. But as the smoke cleared, the organization developed a rigorous testing program to determine the real tar and nicotine content. The tobacco industry was irritated, but the testing protocols became models for the government's own testing program.

With nuclear testing in the 1950s, CU reported that when the cows came home they were bringing with them increasing amounts of deadly Strontium 90. The CU report, "The Milk We Drink," put heat on the dairy industry, the Atomic Energy Commission, and the Public Health Service, and government monitoring was improved.

CU also found that of 39 brands of automobile seat belts available in 1956, 26 failed when their protection was needed most. In the early sixties, it pressed hard for immediate and universal adoption of belts and harnesses. Industry and government have since realized the value of such protection.

In the 1970s, power lawn mowers cut more than grass, accounting for 160,000 injuries a year. At the request of the Consumer Product Safety Commission, CU engineers developed safety standards that were eventually written into law.

When it first tested microwave ovens, Consumers Union found that significant levels of radiation were leaking from the appliances and that safe levels of radiation had not been determined. All tested ovens were rated "Not recommended." Eventually the manufacturers substantially reduced emission levels and warning labels were made mandatory.

Many years ago, Colston Warne, CU's first president, said, "The idea of testing and appraising products by name constitutes an overdue scientific mechanism designed to restore rationality to the marketplace."

Perhaps rationality and the marketplace really constitute a contradiction in terms. Perhaps they can never be united. Perhaps, as Stuart Chase once said, the marketplace will always be a Wonderland and the consumer an Alice lost in it.

Even if that is true, we certainly can take heart that the work of Chase, Arthur Kallet, Colston Warne, and those who have followed them have helped us find our way through that Wonderland. Because of them, more intelligent choices have been made, effective laws passed, resources protected, and lives enriched and saved.

In 1968, at a ceremony marking the signing of a new federal meat inspection law, eighty-nine-year-old Upton Sinclair—only months from his death—said, "There is no end to this fight, is there?"

There is no end, but there is Consumers Union.

In the past. And in the future.

. . . And that's the way it is.

TESTING

Sunburn Preventives

CU tested 15 brands of sunburn preventives for the third issue of *Consumers Union Reports*, later known as *Consumer Reports*. Five staff members volunteered their arms, backs, and abdomens to ultraviolet-ray exposure from both natural sunlight and the light from a mercury arc lamp. Three of the subjects had their backs and abdomens marked off in test sections with black crayon. Each section was covered with a different lotion, then exposed to ultraviolet rays. The other two subjects' arms were used for the test, with adhesive tape separating the areas to which the different lotions were applied. There was complete correlation of the results for each product among the persons tested. The areas covered by two products, Mulsitan and Dorothy Gray Sunburn Cream, showed no burning whatsoever. Ardena Sun-Pruf Cream permitted some penetration, as was evidenced by slight redness of the section it covered. None of the other lotions offered any appreciable protection, and the test subjects complained that the sections these lotions covered were as painful to the touch as completely unprotected areas.

CU felt that one product, Mor-Tan, deserved particular attention. "Its makers promise it will prevent not only sunburn, but also blistering, windburn, freckles, and poison ivy, and relieve hay fever, nose and throat irritations, and external bleeding. If this is not enough, the label informs the prospective buyer that Mor-Tan will cause new skin to grow on burned flesh—and it is an effective mouth wash. . . . Since Mor-Tan is supposed to do practically everything else, the manufacturer feels impelled to add that 'Mor-Tan will not grow hair.' Mor-Tan was not tested for its effects on hair growth, hay fever, or halitosis, but it didn't prevent sunburn," CU wrote.

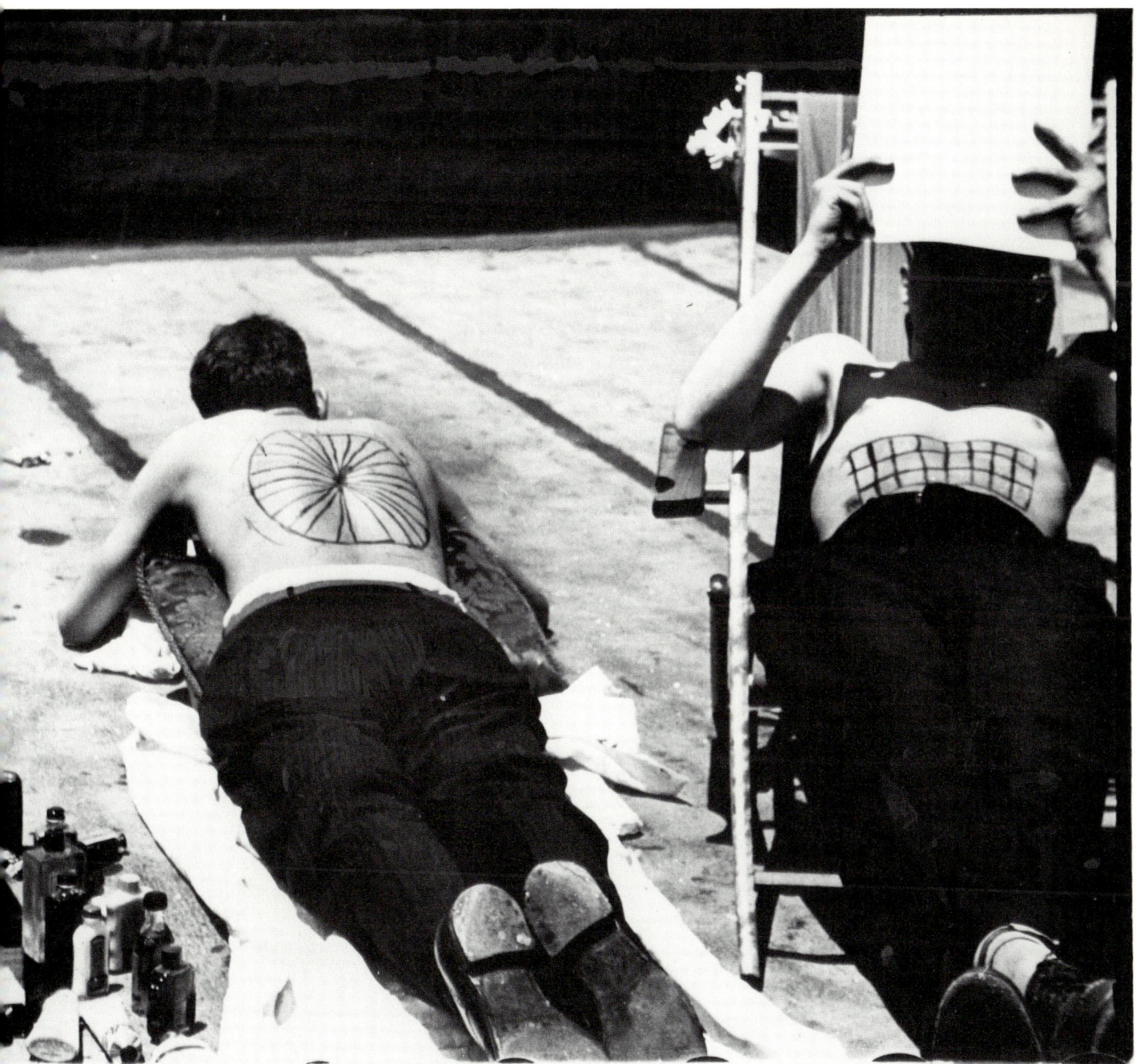

Sunburn Preventives

JULY 1940

This was the fifth year CU tested sunburn preventives. Since 1936, when only two products were rated as providing "good protection," technical progress in perfecting sunscreen chemicals had considerably increased the number of effective brands on the market. By 1939, CU was testing 37 brands, with 13 found to give "good protection." For this report, CU tested 10 of these 13 brands (the other 3 were no longer available). In the 1939 tests, preventives were subjected to both spectrographic testing, in which a beam of sunburn-causing ultraviolet light was passed through a thin film of the preventive, and by skin tests. Since good correlation was found between the two methods, only skin tests (involving actual sun exposure) were made in 1940. Men and women volunteers with both light and dark complexions were used as test subjects. The lotions and creams were applied in a grid pattern, one product per square. The test subjects then permitted their backs to be exposed to the sun for fixed periods of time. Eight products were rated as providing "good protection" two gave only "fair protection."

In recent years, the sunscreen industry has developed a rating system for its products based on a Sun Protection Factor (SPF) number that informs consumers of the degree to which a particular product or formulation will protect skin from burning ultraviolet rays. The SPF rating has made it unnecessary for volunteers to suffer any longer from checkerboard backs.

4

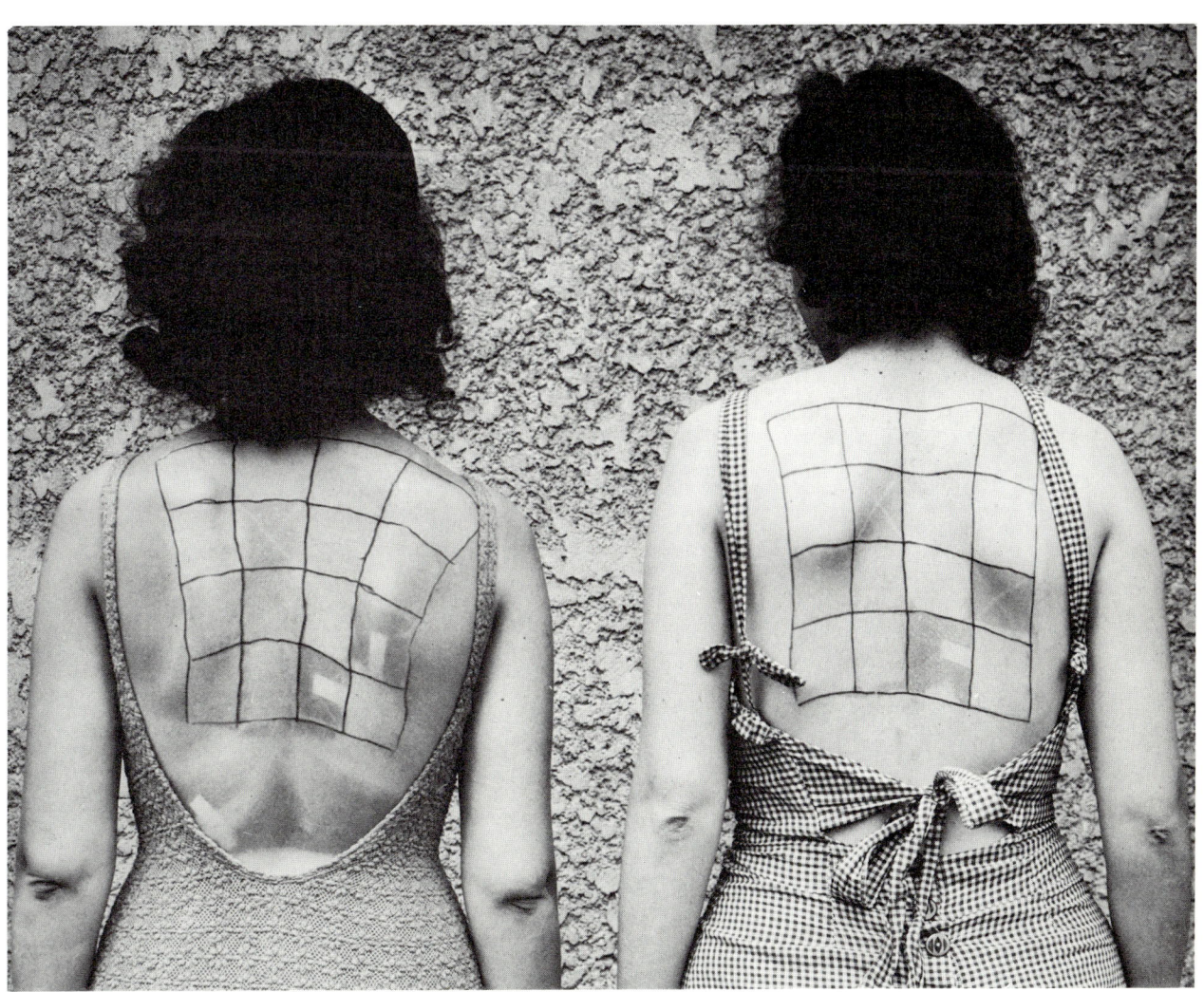

Lipstick

AUGUST 1942

Lipsticks differ in their tendency to leave a permanent stain on fabrics. In one test, a technologist applied lipstick to cotton fabric. Here, laboratory code numbers were used as a key to identify samples being tested for staining tendency. After allowing the lipstick to "set" for a period of time, the fabric was washed in a standardized way for 30 minutes in hot, soapy water to which washing soda had been added. Some stains washed out completely; others did not. Among the worst were Lentheric Bal Masque Brune Satine ($1.00), Almay Dark ($1.10), Associated Distributors Tattoo Pastel ($.49), Colonial Dames Medium ($1.00), L'Adonna Light ($.50), Elizabeth Post Heavenly Pink ($.10), and Pond's Lips Dark Secret ($.10). In all, 63 brands were tested. "While lipstick should adhere to the lips," CU wrote, "it should adhere as little as possible to other things. Catastrophic losses of linens due to lipstick stains have been suffered by hotels and restaurants. No estimate is available of the number of napkins, towels, and pillowcases that have been similarly ruined in homes."

176
110
131
211
205
102
224
202
187
142
167
207
107
212
106
204
128
148
185
200
127
181
182
229
130
108
221
104
114
208
118
168
146
143
210
223
190
158
115
192
133
144
219
199
226
112
164
216
214
206
166
196
119
151
111

Shoes

MARCH 1943

As part of a series of advice articles on how to make things last longer during the period of shortages occasioned by World War II, Consumers Union published a series of do's and don'ts involving shoe care. Here, readers were advised not to put wet shoes on a radiator or in hot sunshine to dry. To do so would injure the leather, causing unsightly curling of the toes. "Instead," CU advised, "stuff the toes with crumpled newspaper, and let the shoes dry slowly, away from direct heat."

Men's Shoes

As of 1943, CU's test of men's shoes was the biggest technical project in its history—and probably the most comprehensive comparative testing of shoes undertaken by any organization. Because this was wartime, CU advised, ". . . don't buy shoes unless you really need them. Although the government allows you nearly three pairs of shoes a year at the present time, that doesn't mean that you're under compulsion to use the full quota. . . . But if you do need shoes there's no reason why the government's allotment shouldn't be adequate. . . . The thing to do is to get the best buy you can afford, which doesn't mean the highest priced one." ▪ One hundred forty-three pairs of 33 different brands of shoes, ranging in price from $2.00 to $22.50, were evaluated. "Not even an expert can tell the quality of a pair of shoes by examining them in a store," CU reported. "To rate shoes, it is necessary to begin by duplicating, in reverse, the steps followed in making the shoe." Each shoe tested was placed on a cobbler's last and dissected down to its essential parts. While it was being torn down, its construction features were noted. Then, each of the main parts was tested to determine the quality of the material from which it was made. First the heel was torn off and examined, then the sole, the shank, uppers, toe box, and vamp. The quarter, counter, and stitching were assessed, along with the strength of the leather. Coward, Shriner Shoe, Florsheim, Stetson, and Nunn-Bush—at $8.95 to $10.85 a pair—were judged to offer the best value for the money in the higher price ranges, with Thom McAn ($4.20) and Towncraft ($4.79) judged Best Buys in the lower price ranges, assuming the shoes felt comfortable. Comfort was one thing that couldn't be checked in the laboratory, either back then—or now.

Gelatin Desserts

APRIL 1945

A panel of "taste testers" evaluated 35 gelatin desserts, including strawberry, raspberry, cherry, lemon, lime, and wine flavors. In each test, three desserts, carefully prepared according to directions and identified only as A, B, and C, were served to tasters who rated their flavors as Good, Fair, or Poor. Tasters were also asked to pass judgment on consistency and sweetness, and to record what they thought was the flavor of each sample. Samples were served four times daily—twice in the morning and twice in the afternoon. All brands were tested at least twice by each taster. When results of the two tests disagreed widely, a third test was made and the results averaged. Despite such variable factors as degree of hunger and "taste fatigue," the judgments of individual tasters remained remarkably consistent. Ninety-two percent of the duplicate tests gave results in agreement with the original. One common finding was that tasters experienced real difficulty in deciding the probable flavor of any given sample of gelatin. When they could see the color, the tasters found it easy to guess the flavor of a yellow lemon or a green lime, but one colored red was equally likely to be called cherry, raspberry, or strawberry. To check this apparent flavor similarity, a small group of tasters was blindfolded and served samples of all flavors. The result was that with the exception of wine flavors, with their distinctive fermented taste, all flavored gelatins of a given brand tasted pretty much alike. Without the visual stimulus of color, even some lemons or limes were mistaken for strawberry.

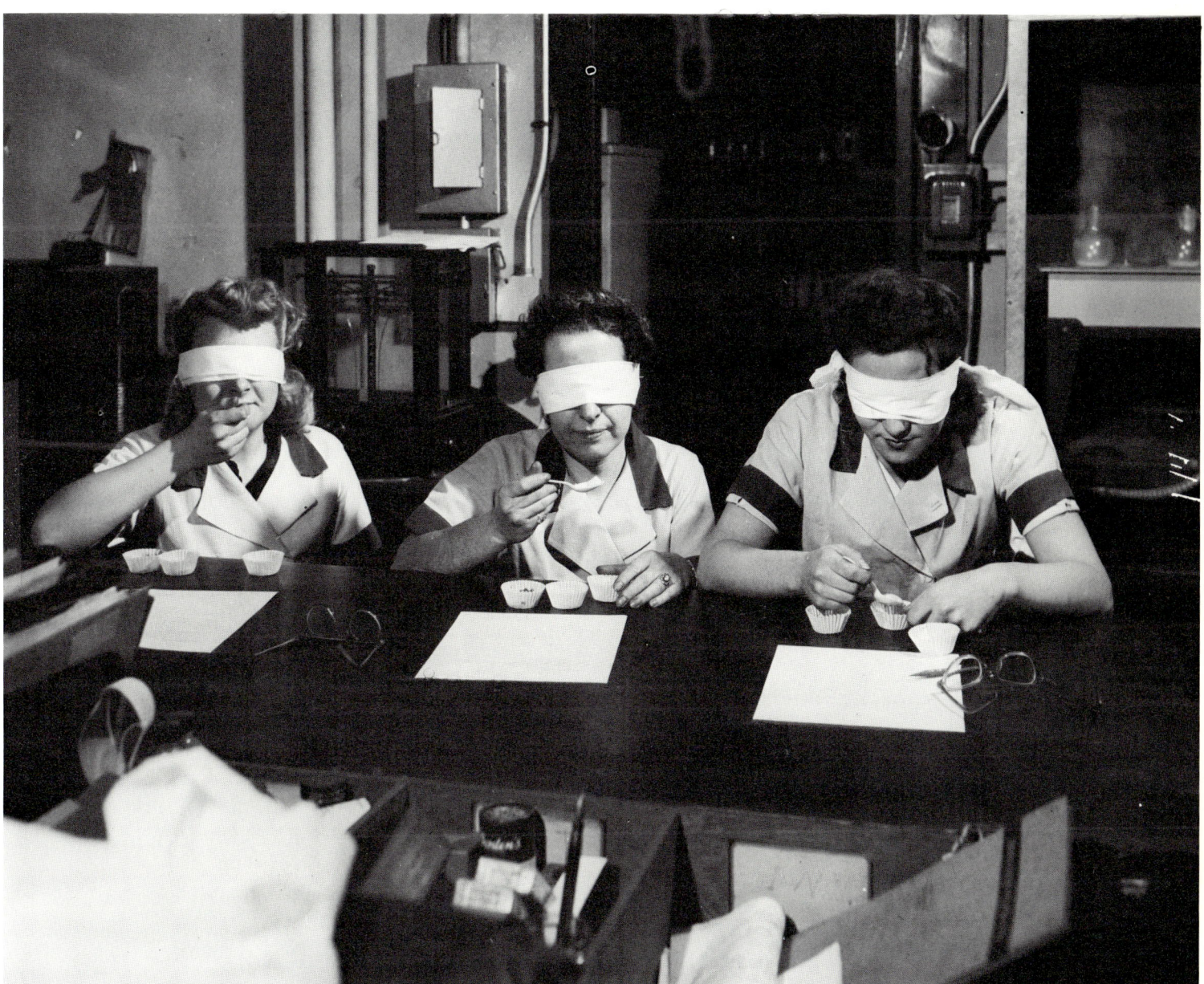

Canned Asparagus

MAY 1945

CU found that 1945 was a good year for canned asparagus. Fifty-nine brands were tested for CU by U.S. Department of Agriculture graders for tenderness, absence of defects, color, and clearness of liquor. Since asparagus stalks can be stringy and tough, tenderness was considered the most important factor, accounting for 40 percent of the total score. Fifty-two brands were judged U.S. Grade A or Fancy. Only one brand was Substandard. Asparagus points, as defined in government grades, measured less than 2¾ inches (left); tips were 2¾ to 3¾ inches long (center); and spears (right) were longer than 3¾ inches. Asparagus was expensive, even in 1945, with the highest priced canned variety, green spears, priced at $.40 to $.75 per pound (drained weight).

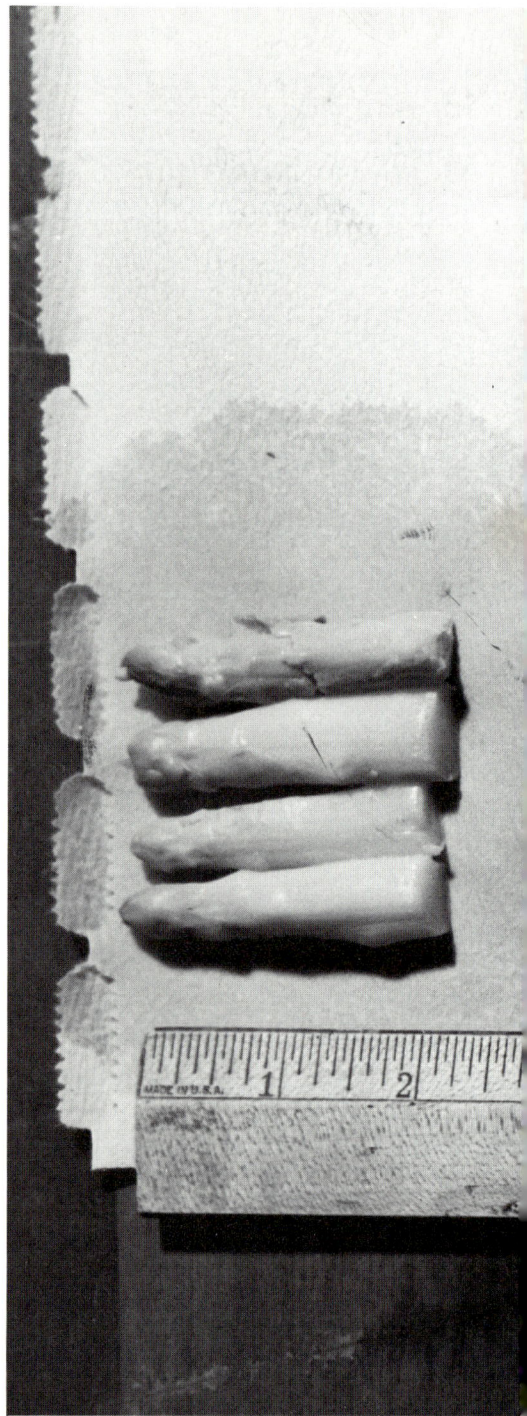

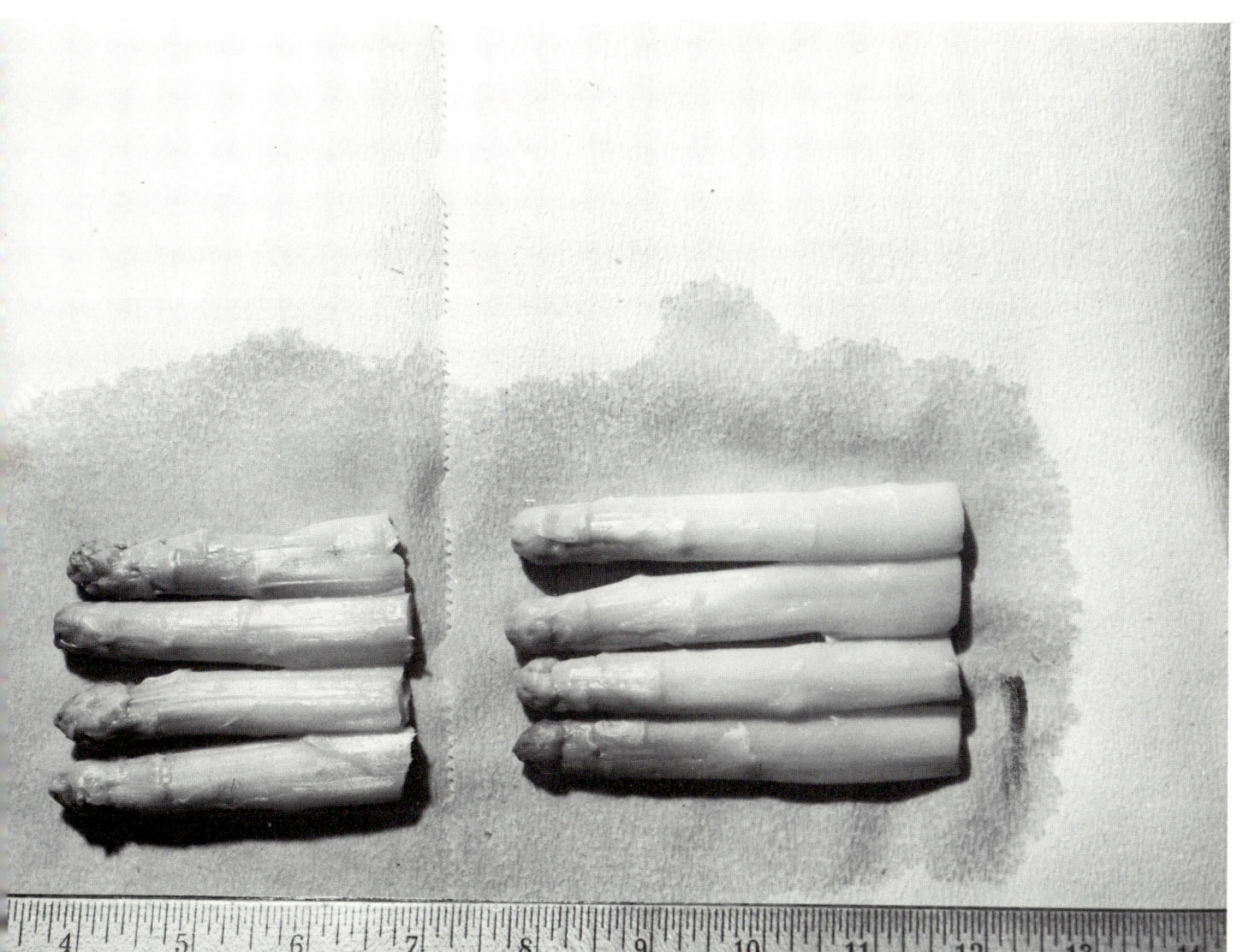

Lipstick

JANUARY 1946

Three to five colors of 27 brands of lipstick were examined for odor (quality and strength), color, ease of application, consistency, adherence, softening point, sweating, and staining on cotton. Here, a cosmetics expert evaluates several samples for odor, color, consistency, and adherence—qualities not measurable by laboratory tests. Only four brands—Tangee, Dorothy Gray, Photo Finish, and Yardley—were judged satisfactory from color to color in the three properties considered most important by experts: ease of application, consistency, and adherence.

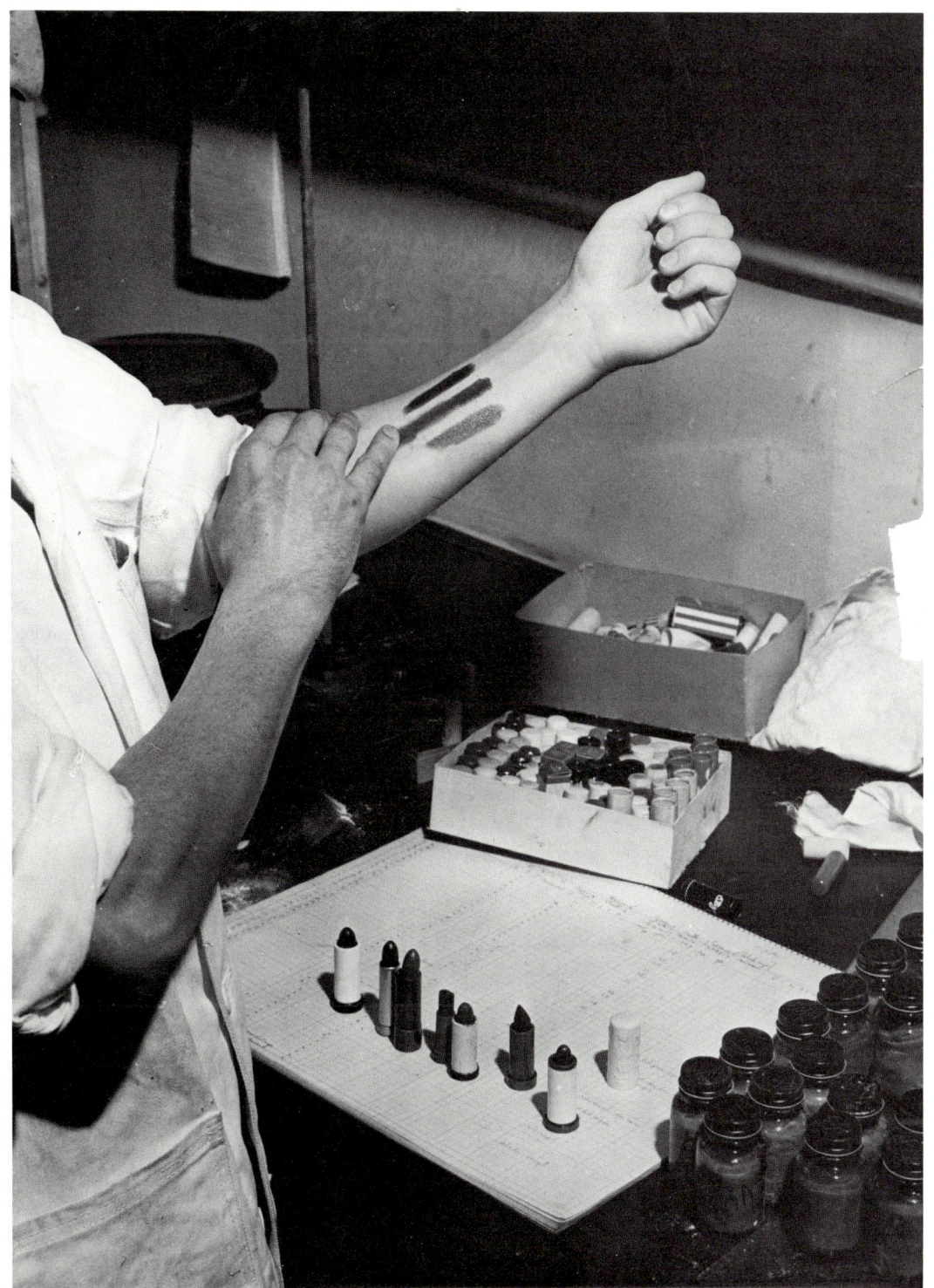

Men's Shoes

OCTOBER 1948

Durability testing often requires engineers to devise simulated use patterns that accelerate the wear and tear a product receives under normal conditions. The machine shown here flexed strips of leather from the vamps of 52 brands and styles of men's shoes, 4 at a time, until they broke. "Frequently the first sign of wear in an inferior shoe is the creasing or cracking of the leather in the vamp, which is flexed every time you take a step," CU wrote. The number of flexings each sample withstood was therefore an important factor in the shoe's rating. The sample at the upper right broke after only 113 flexings, as indicated by the reading on the counting device. CU rated shoes in this project only for characteristics likely to affect wearing quality; no consideration was given to style factors or to range of sizes available.

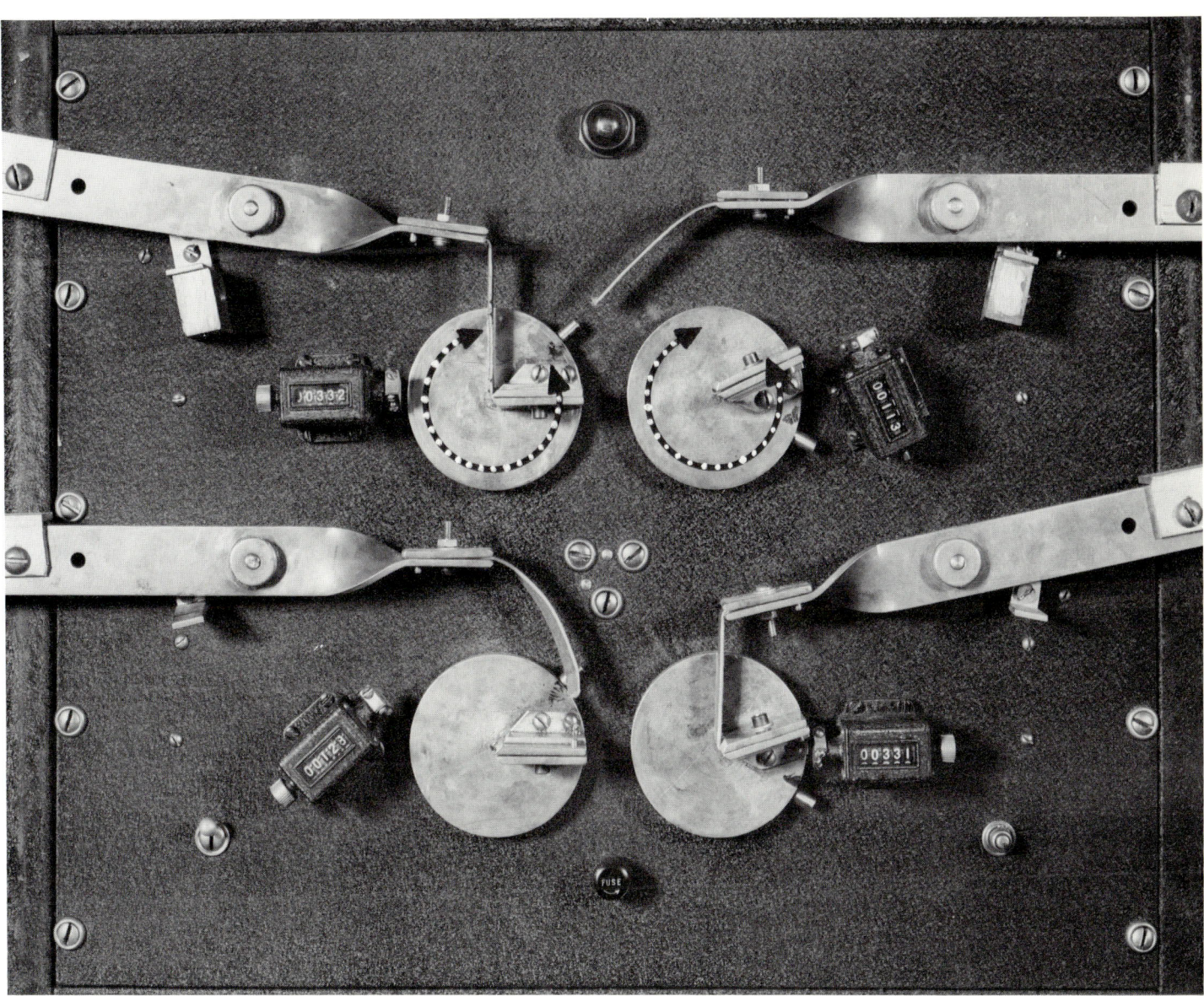

Tire Gauges

MARCH 1949

Extra-low-pressure (ELP) tires were virtually standard equipment on all 1949 cars. CU recommended checking the tires every week or two to spot slow leaks, since even a slight (two or three pounds) departure from the recommended pressure could result in a shortened life, poor performance, even tire failure. Given these circumstances, an accurate tire gauge was essential to good tire care.

According to CU, a gauge should be accurate within two pounds in any weather. In this test, a technician checks a pencil-type gauge in a temperature-controlled room. He is measuring the gauge's reading against a round master gauge of known accuracy at 38°F, 72°F, and 110°F, by pressing its business end against a tire valve set into an air tank pressurized by a remote air compressor. The tester is dressed for the wintry environment being simulated for the test in progress.

Several gauges proved inaccurate at this coldest temperature, and at other test temperatures as well. Eight samples of each brand were tested; only two brands met CU's standards of accuracy in all samples tested.

Ballpoint Pens

JUNE 1949

When Consumers Union took its first look at ballpoint pens in 1946, soon after their introduction, the average price of 22 brands was $9.00. Manufacturers made much of their supposed long writing life—"normal 5 to 15 years supply of ink," one claimed—but few pens fared well in CU's tests. In 1949, CU tested the writing life of ballpoint pens by operating them on a moving paper strip that was fed through this machine at a uniform rate. Each pen was weighted to simulate the pressure applied to the tip in normal use. The test pens revolved slowly while continuously describing circles on the paper, until the ink supply was used up or the pen stopped writing for other reasons. Acceptable pens had average writing times ranging from 8 hours (price, $.98) to 65 hours (price $1.00), depending on the brand and model.

Refrigerators

JUNE 1949

These fourteen single-door refrigerators are ready for the test line. Models were tested for their ability to maintain sufficiently cold inside temperatures under simulated midsummer conditions outside, and for their operating economy (ranging from $1.30 to $3.35 per month at 1949 utility prices). CU engineers evaluated insulation, tested surface finishes, and measured the ability of freezer compartments to make ice. All of these refrigerators had small freezers—most of which stayed well above 32°F—but at that time the limited amount of frozen food available commercially was generally either used upon purchase or in a somewhat thawed state the next day.

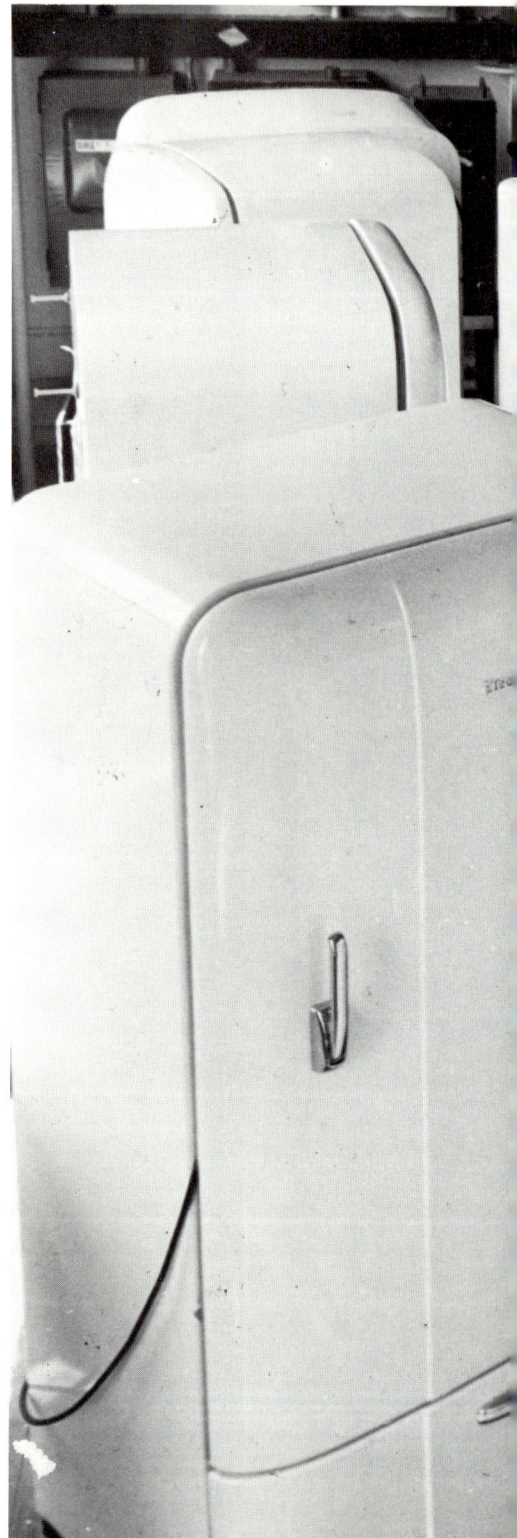

Toothpaste and Tooth Powder

AUGUST 1949

"Few dentifrices are advertised as the simple cleaning preparations most of them are," CU wrote in 1949, before the widespread use of fluorides in toothpastes. "Instead, their makers talk about alkalizing, sweetening the breath, banishing 'tobacco mouth,' hardening the gums, whitening the teeth, and giving first aid to victims of halitosis, acidosis, gingivitis, bleeding gums, and other ailments for which a dentist or doctor rather than a toothpaste is required."

For this report, CU tested 44 popular brands of toothpaste and 49 brands of tooth powder, to determine, first of all, abrasiveness and the presence of grit. (Several brands were rated Not Acceptable because they contained particles that were hard enough to scratch glass.) Other tests were performed for degree of acidity or alkalinity, presence of some harmful or potentially harmful substances, extrusion, consistency, stability, texture, and limited use tests were made for flavor, odor, and possibly irritating effects. Here consistency is checked by extruding a small amount of paste from the tube and measuring with a stopwatch the time it took to drop. All the regular pastes met the federal specification for consistency except Pepsodent, Sears Dent-A-Mint, and TMC; these were somewhat thin, but not so thin as to make them unsatisfactory to use.

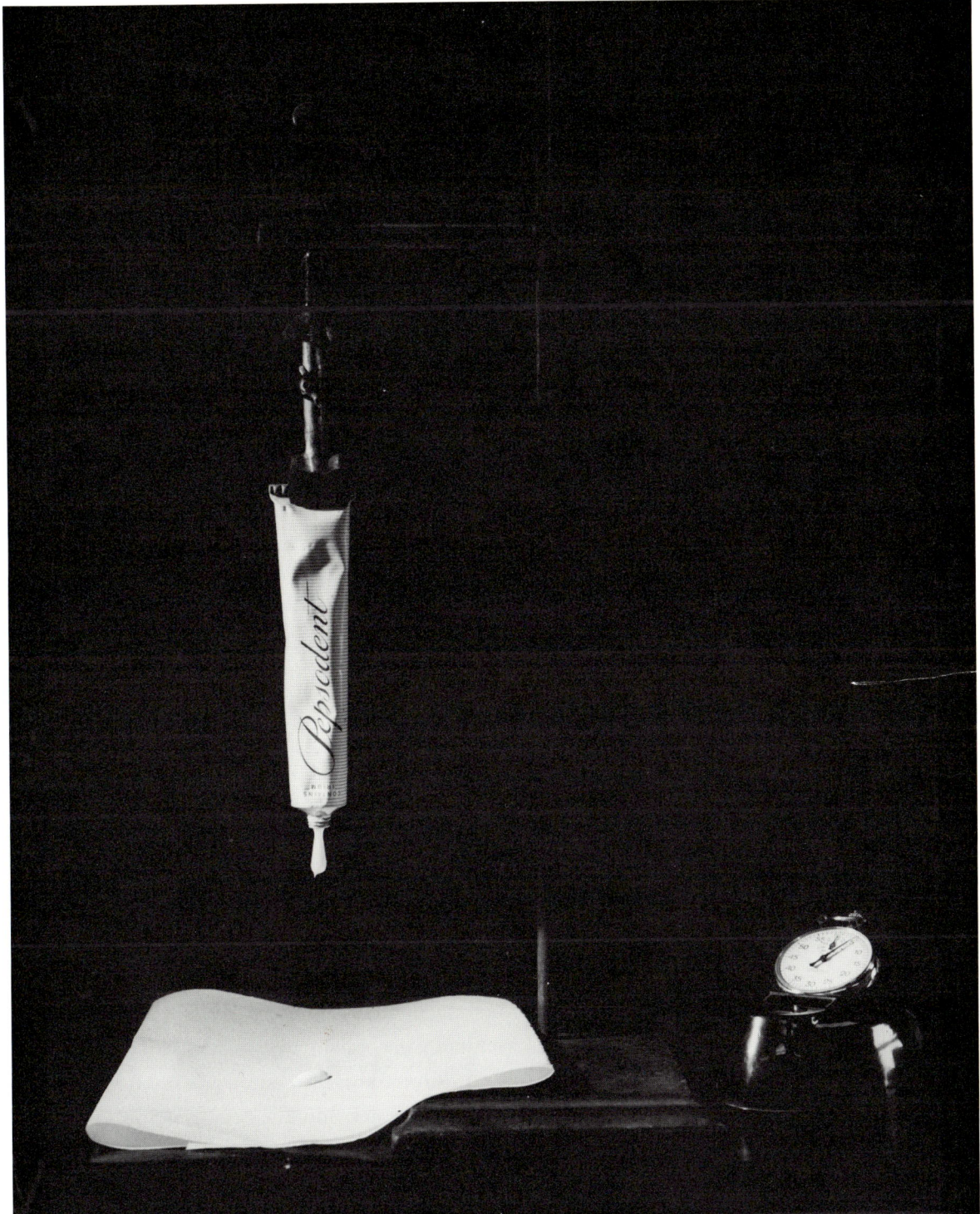

Inks

I n the days when pens had to be filled regularly from the ink bottle, ink's washability was of prime consideration to consumers. The permanence of "permanent" writing ink was also important when writing had to be preserved for long periods.

CU tested 34 blue, black, and blue-black permanent and washable inks with writing samples and these ink streaks, produced by flowing measured portions of each brand over white bond paper held at a 45-degree angle.

According to CU, good writing ink should flow uniformly from the pen and produce even lines that do not "feather" (spread out at the edges) or bleed through the paper to obscure writing on the other side. But CU's major ink tests were designed to find out how well the various brands lived up to their claims for permanence or washability. In one test, technicians soaked ink streaks in water overnight. Submersion removed most "washable" ink, they found, but truly "permanent" ink was not affected. In another test, pieces of cotton and wool cloth were spotted with samples of the various "washable" inks and then laundered twice in an automatic washing machine. All of the washable blue inks were found to be truly washable. However, the washable black inks left stains on wool or cotton, or both, and were rated Not Acceptable.

Automatic Record Changer #1

APRIL 1950

In June 1948, CU had introduced plans for a high-fidelity AM/FM radio phonograph that could be assembled from readily available components for about $150, plus the cost of the cabinet. CU's complete, illustrated instructions sold for $.50, and many thousands of *Consumer Reports* readers and their friends built these custom sets.

As originally described, the custom-built combination used a Webster single-speed (78 rpm) record changer. Within two years, however, records were no longer all running at one speed. For the more complicated requirements of the three speeds, three diameters, two-groove widths, and two center-hole sizes, CU ran tests on the Webster 356-27 record changer, the first multispeed changer on the market.

Two samples of the changer were wired to a single loudspeaker. A panel of trained listeners then compared sound quality between a record that had been subjected to repeated playings with the Webster changer and a brand-new sample of the same record, played alternately through changer-amplifier A, then changer-amplifier B. The amplifiers used in this test were Bell 2122s—the same ones recommended for CU's custom-designed sound system.

Automatic Record Changer #2

APRIL 1950

CU tested ten Webster samples for record wear by loading three with ten 12-inch 78s, three with ten 7-inch 45s, and three with two 12-inch 33s, so that a full cycle would occupy approximately 37 minutes of playing time, regardless of record type. One sample was maintained as a standard of comparison. Records of five major manufacturers were used in the tests to allow for possible variations in surface characteristics, materials, and groove shapes. Changers were carefully leveled and needle pressure checked before the tests, and needles were examined under a microscope to eliminate those that showed irregularities. At regular intervals, the records being tested were compared in controlled listening tests (see previous photo) with brand new pressings of the same numbers, and any distortion, groove breakdown, or increase of background noise, crackle, or rattling was noted. In general, the tests showed the Webster to be quite satisfactory with respect to record wear.

Nonautomatic Washing Machines

JUNE 1950

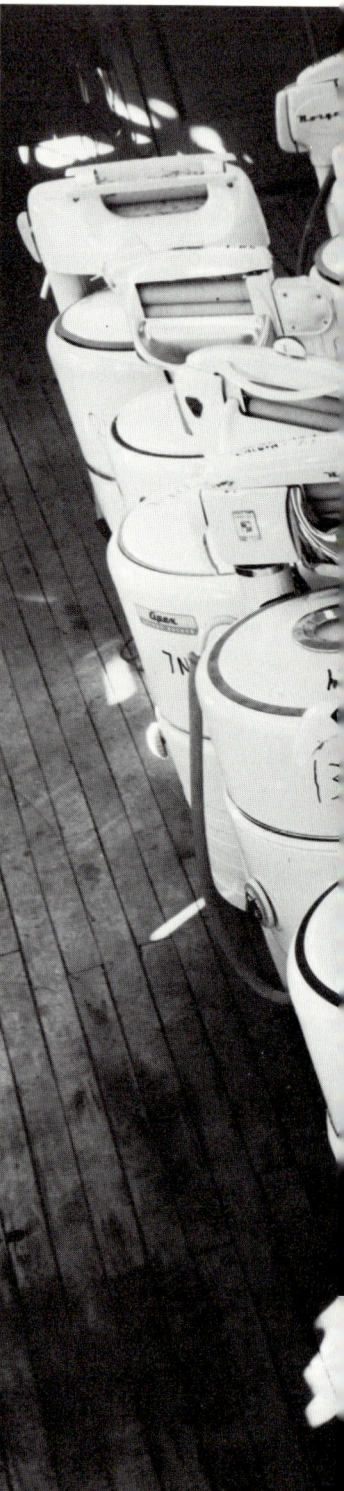

While fully automatic and semiautomatic washing machines were widely available by this time, the major drawback for many consumers was their high price. A second drawback was that these automatics took up permanent floor space, whereas nonautomatic machines could be rolled away and conveniently stored. Some automatic models even had to be bolted down.

CU tested 20 nonautomatic machines with power wringers in the $90 to $185 price range. (Comparable semiautomatic machines could cost from $170 to $200, and fully automatic models could run as high as $370.) Of the 20 models tested, 10 were rated Not Acceptable because of poor durability, hazardous wringer mechanisms, or because clothes tended to become caught or abraded under the agitator. The highest rated machine, the $184.95 Maytag, was also the most expensive, but 7 others, all rated Good, were considerably less costly.

Canned Green Beans

SEPTEMBER 1950

CU shoppers in 22 cities purchased 508 cans of green beans, including 5 or 6 samples of each brand. U.S. Department of Agriculture graders tested a total of 53 brands for CU in conformance with official standards. In CU's can-coding room, each can's original label was removed and the can relabeled with a code number to hide brand identity before going off to the laboratory for grading. Absence of defects and the youngness of the beans (which largely determines their tenderness) were the main factors in the grading. All brands were found to be Acceptable.

Automobile Tires

SEPTEMBER–NOVEMBER 1950

CU decided to subject automobile tires to actual road-wear tests on the basis of the experts' virtually unanimous opinion that laboratory tests are unreliable. These four new Fords, identical except for color, were driven back and forth through Texas over a 200-mile route running from San Antonio to Hico. The cars made two round trips daily, for a total of 800 miles per car. The purpose of the test was to subject the 16 tires on the cars to 12,800 miles of actual road wear under carefully controlled conditions. The brakes were equalized, and each wheel was aligned and balanced. Weights were distributed so that, with each driver seated and the gasoline tank half full, each tire carried 1,100 pounds. The cars never separated from each other by more than half a mile. If one car stopped for any reason, all four stopped. The first and last cars of the cavalcade were equipped with recording tachometers that made a permanent record of all stops and of speed variations along the route. Tires were rotated so that each tire traveled 800 miles on each of the 16 wheels. Tires were weighed at the start of the tests and again at 800-mile intervals to determine how much tread was lost. In general, the conditions of the test (overloaded tires, higher-than-average driving speeds, midsummer Texas temperatures, and so forth) were of a type likely to result in relatively rapid tire wear. Analysis of the test results indicated that conditions were in fact very well controlled.

Plastic Dishes #1

JANUARY 1951

Plastic dishes are much harder to break than ceramics, but they tend to scratch more easily and can have other problems as well. In order to develop a test for scratch resistance, CU technicians first determined how hard different people pushed downward with the knife when they cut meat. This scale measured the force most people exerted on the knife alone as varying from about three to five pounds (for tough meat). For scratch tests, an average force of four pounds was used. Dishes made of polystyrene plastic were found to be most susceptible to scratching. Melamine dishes—first produced as an answer to the navy's problem with inordinate breakage of seagoing china—did quite well in the tests.

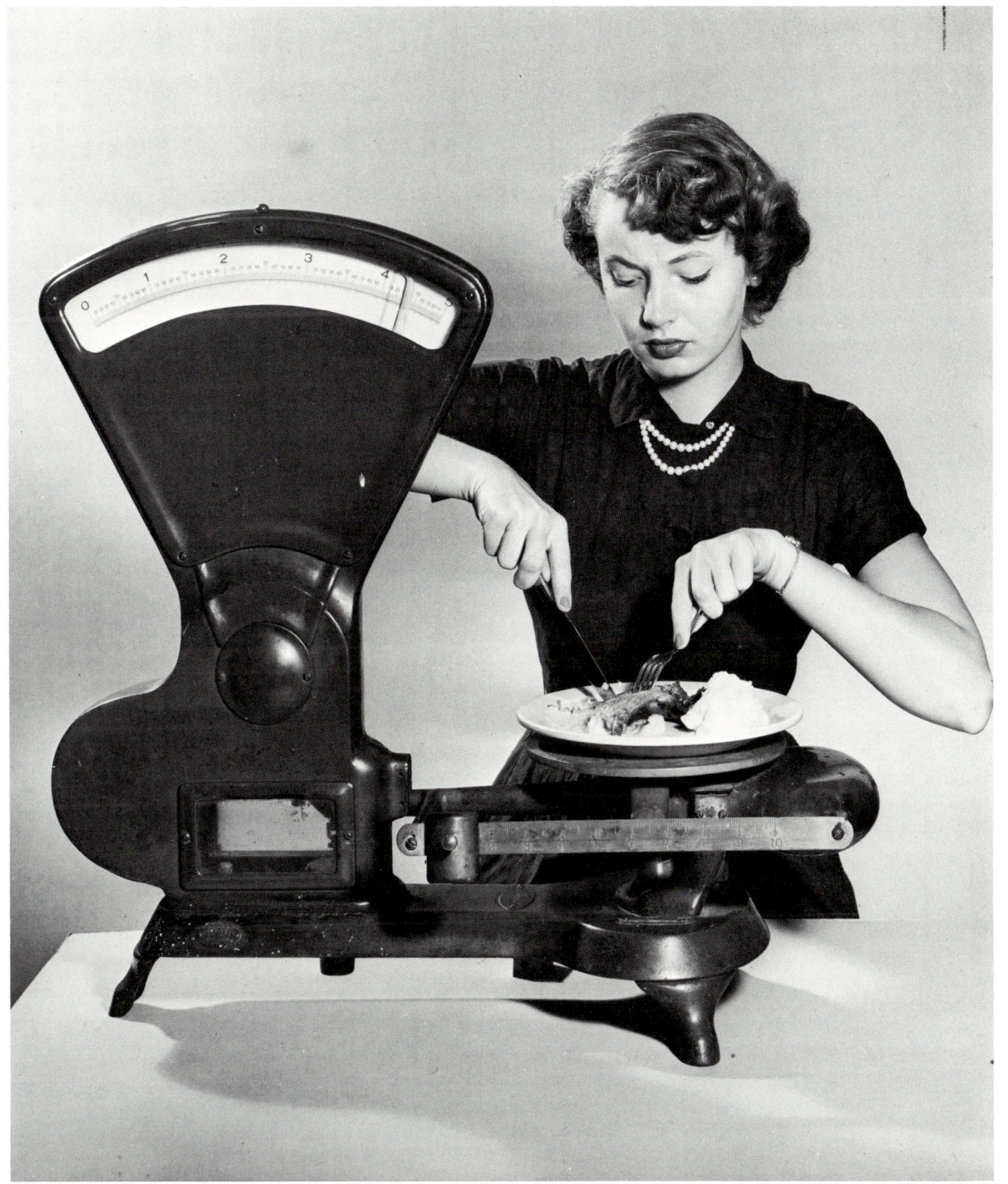

Plastic Dishes #2

JANUARY 1951

This Steri-lite polystyrene plastic cup began to soften when it was immersed in water heated above 170°F, raising the question: What would happen if it was filled with very hot coffee or tea? After spending five minutes in boiling water (under hypothetical sterilization conditions) the cup melted to little more than a blob.

Automatic Electric Steam Irons

OCTOBER 1951

CU was not impressed with the technical quality of this newly introduced product—nine out of eleven models tested were rated Not Acceptable, seven on the grounds that they presented burn or scald hazards; one, the Silex pictured here, because it did so badly in durability tests. One model, which was not a steam iron but a steam attachment only, failed to produce steam properly and gave off a persistent bad odor. Each iron was run daily for 22 hours at a time, followed by a two-hour cooling interval, until a total of 500 heating hours had elapsed. Soleplate temperature and variations were measured at the beginning and end of the heating tests. The thermostat controls of two samples of the Silex iron failed during the tests, resulting in severe overheating and consequent melting of the soleplate.

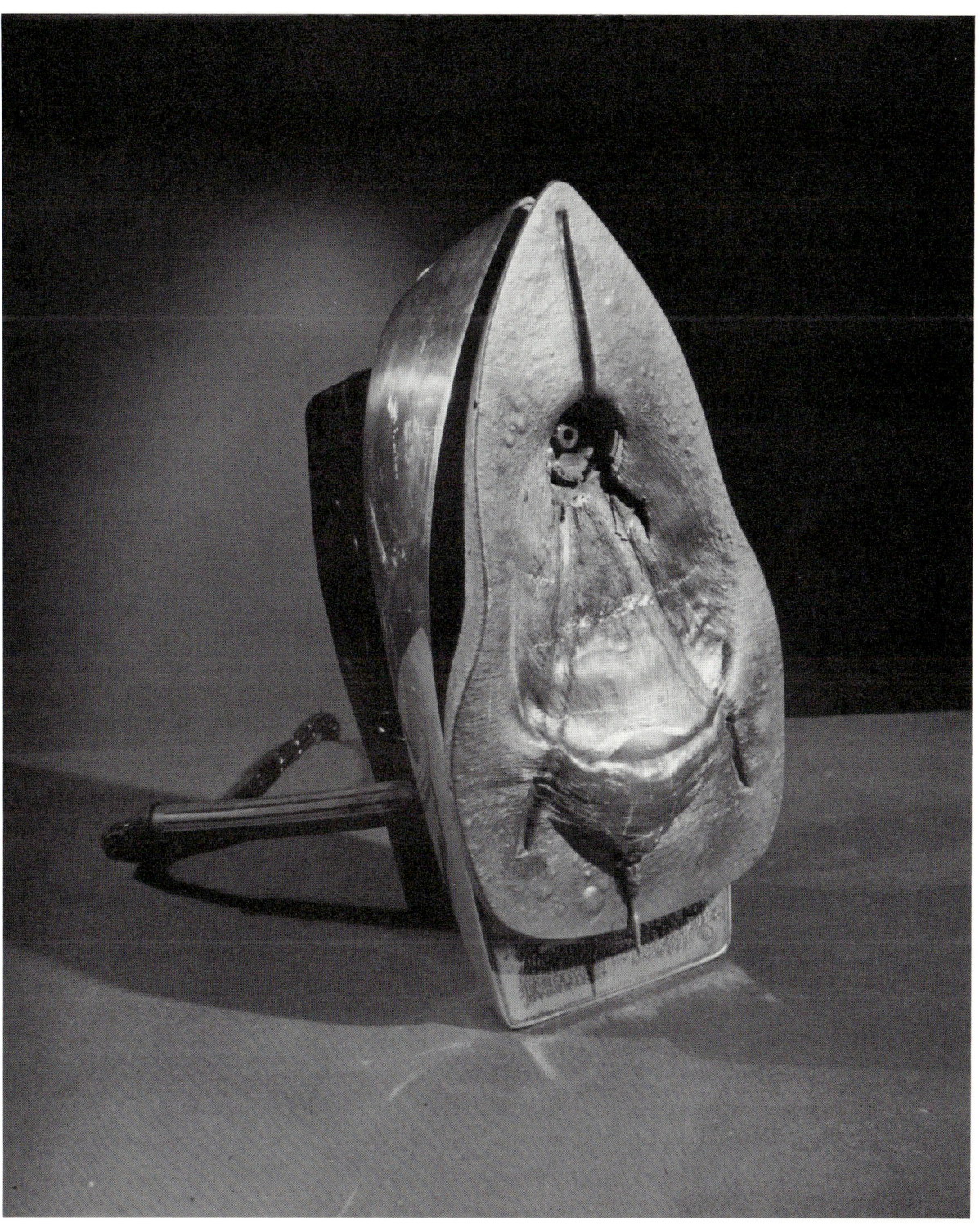

Vaporizers

JANUARY 1952

By 1952, the old-fashioned croup kettle and the steaming tea kettle, formerly much in evidence in sickrooms, were being replaced by electric vaporizers. But the principle of providing a mantle of warm, moist air around the patient was the same, and, as CU pointed out, "from the medical point of view, one method of steam production is as good as another."

"A simple way to create a 'steam tent,' " CU advised, ". . . is to prop up an open umbrella in bed and drape a sheet over the top of the umbrella. Have the vaporizer spout turned so that it pours steam into the tent." Just in case you belonged to one of those households that was thinking of replacing an old-fashioned kettle with a modern electric vaporizer, CU tested 18 models for performance and safety; 11 Acceptable vaporizers were found, at prices ranging from $2.50 to $14.95.

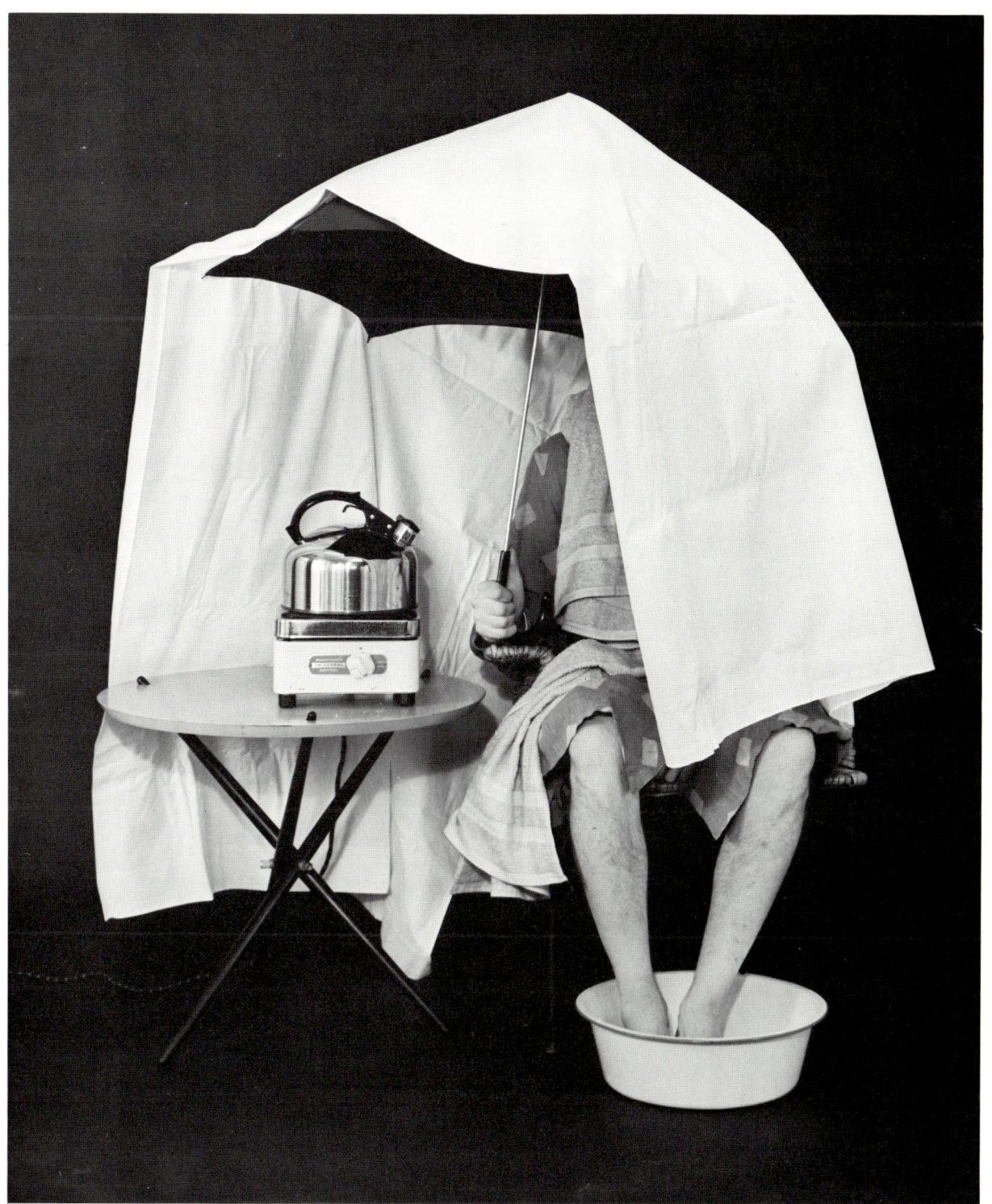

Combs

FEBRUARY 1952

T his "thumb" test, which CU, like the U.S. government, used to test the teeth strength of combs, is quite simple. The back of the comb is held in the curled fingers of the hand and pressure is applied against the fine teeth by the thumb. The test simulates one of the ways the comb's teeth are actually pulled when hair is being combed. Of 71 brands and models tested, 40 combs failed the thumb test. Acceptable combs had at least fair workmanship, passable stiffness, good teeth strength, fairly good back strength, and good durability.

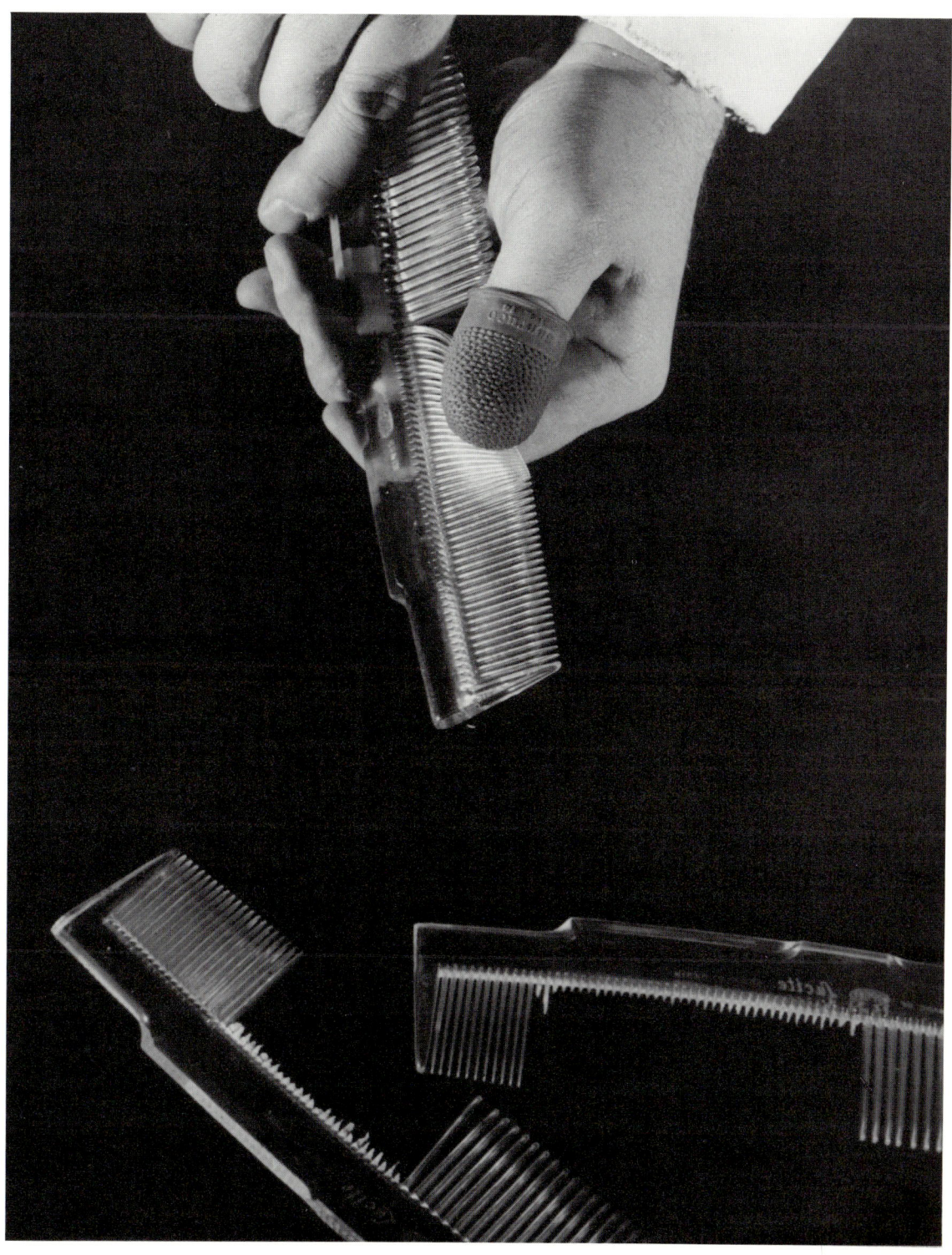

Automobiles

I n 1953, CU rated all standard American models of four-door, five- or six-passenger sedans; two-door sedans that had no four-door counterparts; and station wagons and utility vehicles selling for less than $2,100 at the factory. The fourteen newly purchased cars assembled for this photo would undergo road tests that included: measuring their weight, weight distribution, and interior dimensions; odometer accuracy on a measured mile; handling and performance over a 16-mile course of rough, twisting blacktop road; speedometer accuracy; measuring braking distance; and checking for drag on an incline. The cars would be driven over all types of roads with varying loads and at varying speeds for 2,000 miles. Their gasoline consumption would be measured at constant speeds on level roads and also under simulated traffic conditions. They would be tested for performance and handling while starting, stopping, backing, and climbing a 14 percent grade. Their cornering characteristics would be compared on a variety of curves. Each car would be driven and evaluated by a panel of carefully chosen experts testing for acceleration, hill-climbing ability, and for the effect of heat on their brakes on a 9 percent 1-mile-long grade.

Sunburn Preventives

JULY 1953

In a modification of earlier tests (see "Sunburn Preventives," July 1936 and July 1940), 44 volunteers had their backs sectioned off into patterns of 1-inch squares with photographers' masking tape. A thin film of sunscreen was applied to each square. The subject's back was then exposed to ultraviolet lamps for varying times, depending on each individual's skin coloration and previous experience with sunburn. However, each exposure period was sufficient to produce noticeable burning of the uncovered control areas. The pattern of sunscreen application was varied from one individual to another so as to have each sunburn preventive applied to a different portion of each back (some areas being possibly more sensitive to sun than others). The photograph shows an experimental procedure in which the electrical resistance of the subject's skin was measured to help determine the appropriate length of exposure to the sunlamps. Most of CU's test subjects got good protection from 8 of the 40 brands tested.

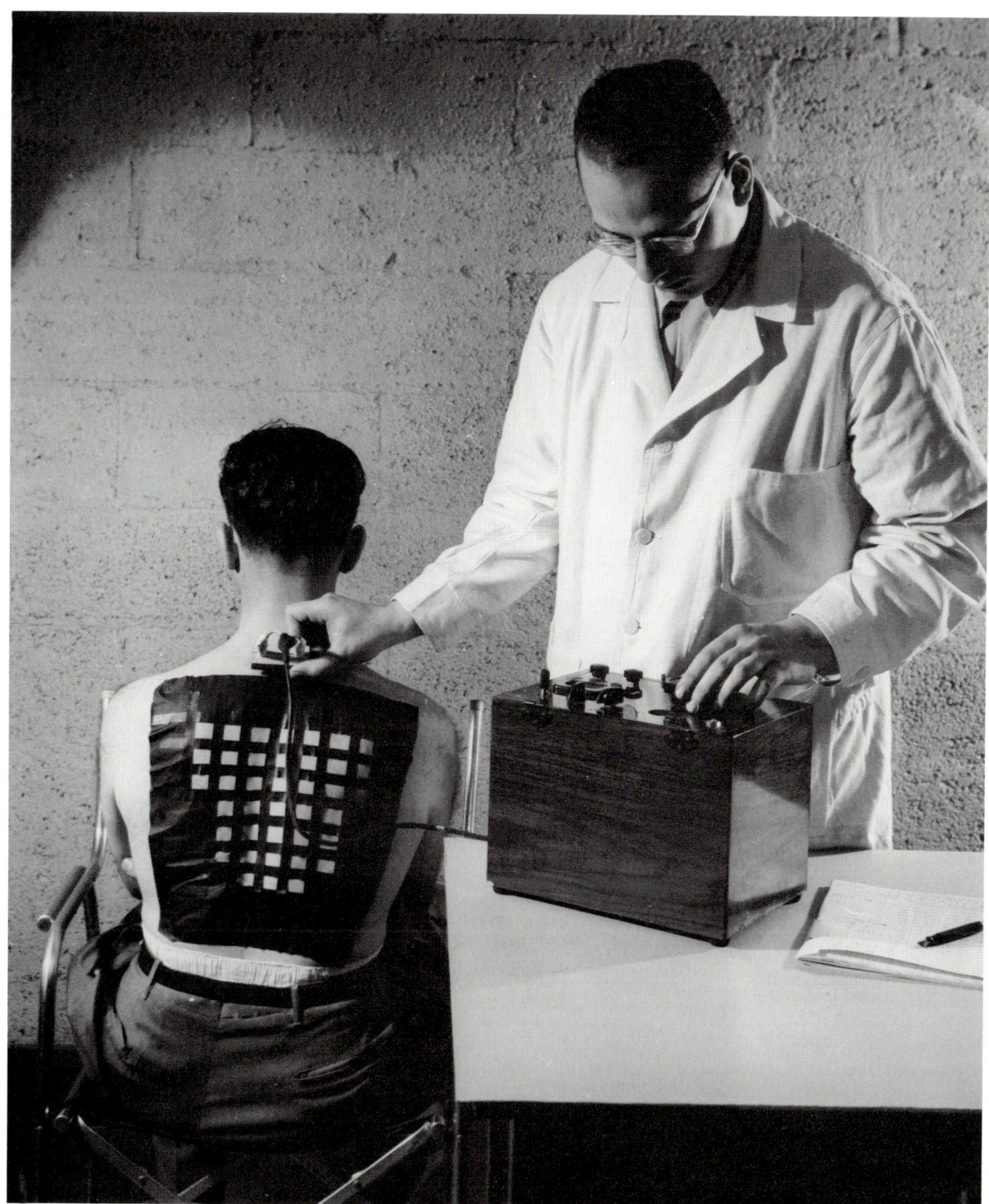

Electric Blankets

JANUARY 1954

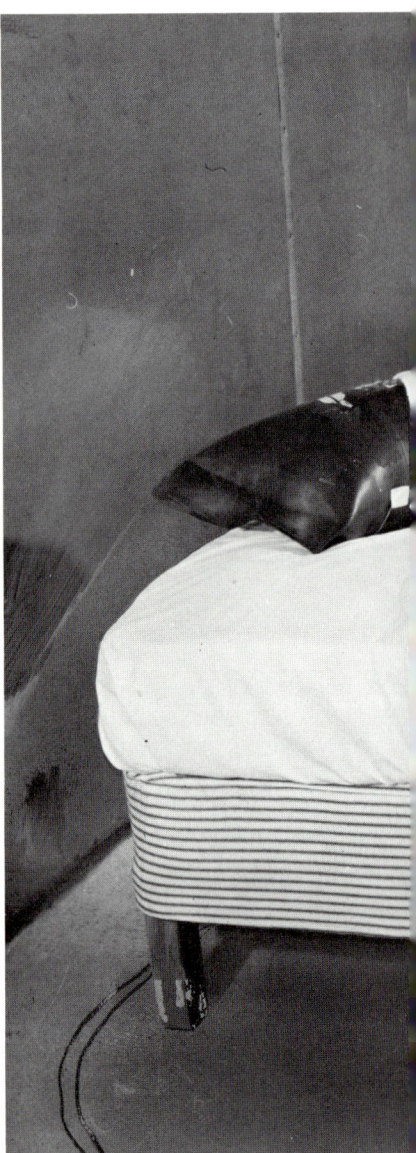

Apeek through the windows of CU's controlled temperature and humidity room during the months this test took place would have revealed two ordinary beds, and in them two recumbent figures, cozily covered, and apparently sound asleep. A look under the covers, however, would have shown the pajama-clad occupants of the beds, Patricia and Ignazio, to be strange creatures. The water-filled dummies, fashioned from inner tubes, maintained an internal temperature of 98°F to 100°F. Like humans, their "skins" dissipated inside heat to the surroundings. In the artificially controlled environment of the test chamber, Ignazio, pictured here, could well have been dreaming of Patricia (not shown), but he was remarkably alert to temperature changes. When an electric blanket failed to keep any part of him warm, he reacted by recording the temperature drop through thermocouples that were attached all over his body. (The wires in the photograph run from the thermocouples to a recording instrument; blanket is folded back.) Meters indicate the amount of electrical energy used by each blanket and the length of time the test has been running. Each blanket's bedside control box is on the table with the other instruments.

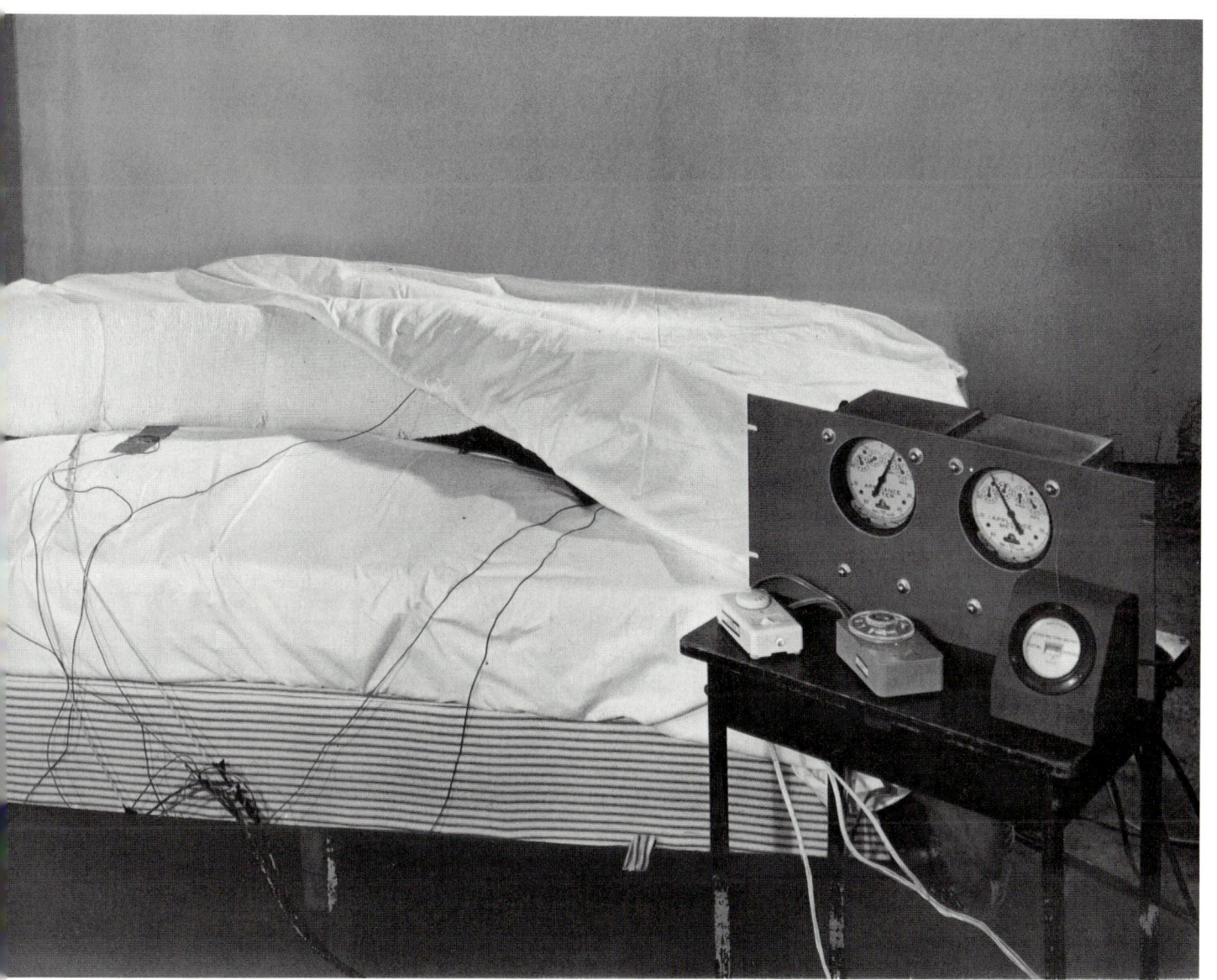

Prolonging the Life of Cut Flowers

JUNE 1954

CU's laboratory tests disclosed that aspirin, a traditional "home remedy" used to retard wilting of cut flowers, is actually a flop as a flower preservative. Instead of extending flower life, adding aspirin to the water substantially reduced the life of many flowers. Here, roses with plain water (left) survived far better than the flowers in water to which aspirin had been added. Commercial flower-preserving chemicals varied in their effectiveness, but all helped extend bloom life to some degree, at least for some flowers.

Shampoos

JANUARY 1955

"Just how clean should a good shampoo leave your hair?" CU asked in 1955. For manageability, most experts agree the hair needs a small amount of oil, either natural oils not removed by the shampoo, or oil added to the hair after it has been cleaned thoroughly. To test 36 brands of shampoo, CU measured how oil affects hair's manageability by immersing clean, oil-free locks of hair in various concentrations of oil in solution. The oil left on the hair after evaporation of the solvent ranged from none (left) to almost 5 percent (right) of the weight of the hair. Each swatch was then combed and an attempt made to form a smooth lock with no loose strands. At the low oil levels, the hair was quite unmanageable; as the oil content increased, the hair became more manageable up to a point. Beyond that, although the hair was manageable, it felt greasy. Regardless of oil content, hair that was completely free of dirt had good gloss, while very dirty hair acquired a "patent leather" look.

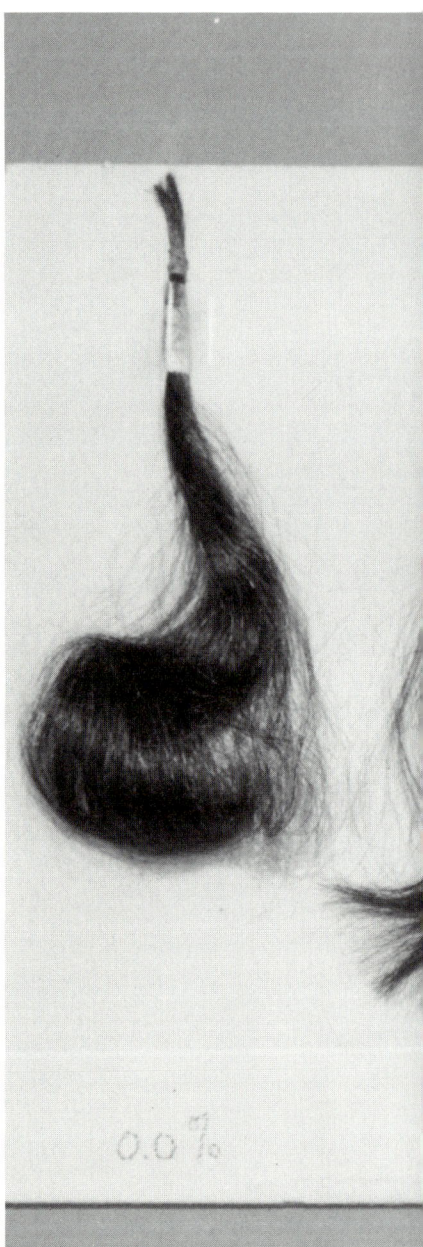

.1%   0.3%   0.6%   1.2%   5%

Antifog Preparations

OCTOBER 1955

A variety of liquid, cream, and impregnated cloth commercial preparations were tested to see whether they prevented fog from forming on glass, whether they cleared glass that was already fogged, how long their effectiveness lasted, and whether they worked on a surface slightly soiled with an oily dirt, as windshields so frequently are. The tests were done using 5-gallon glass containers filled with cracked ice. The outer surface was divided into panels, and all products were tested simultaneously, with one panel left untreated for comparison.

The glass container was placed in a controlled temperature and humidity room at 70°F with 90 percent relative humidity. The "fog" that these preparations were designed to eliminate is the result of a well-known physical phenomenon: cold air won't hold as much moisture as warm air. When warm humid air strikes a cold glass surface, some of its moisture is deposited on the glass. Since water has "surface tension," the water forms tiny droplets that cluster as "fog," dimming visibility through the glass. The antifogging agents lowered the surface tension so that the droplets would spread and coalesce into a continuous clear film of water. Of the 12 preparations tested, however, 4 were either completely ineffective in CU's tests, or prevented fogging for no more than five minutes under test conditions. The other 8 preparations performed better, but did not perform consistently.

All of the commercial preparations had limited distribution. At the time CU purchased its samples, most of the brands were available in only a single city of the 12 large cities shopped. In lieu of the commercial antifoggers, CU recommended several household products that are known to reduce surface tension: bar soap, soap powder, synthetic detergent, shaving cream, and shampoo. "To use the household products, all you need to do is smear a small amount onto the glass surface, then wipe it clear."

Automatic Toasters

MAY 1956

CU used some machines and instruments to test 22 automatic electric toasters, but the Ratings were based primarily on the subjective judgments of CU's engineering staff. Before testing commenced they examined 11 brands of sliced white bread. The brand finally selected appeared to vary least from day to day and from loaf to loaf. Loaves of this bread were purchased daily direct from the baker (more than 6,000 slices were used in the course of the test) and stored for twenty-four hours to permit the bread to "settle" before using it. Any bread left over at the end of each test day was distributed to the CU staff. A new twenty-four-hour-old batch was used for the next day's tests. Degree of brownness, uniformity of color, and convenience factors—accessibility of controls, ease of removing small pieces, size of the toasting chamber—all determined by subjective judgment, were among the most important factors in the Ratings. No toaster could produce slices of toast that were perfectly uniform in color. At best, the slices had patches that were somewhat light or dark. Toasters were also tested for single-slice toasting, safety, and durability, among other factors.

Electric Frying Pans

AUGUST 1956

By 1956, electric frying pans were nothing new—Westinghouse had one on the market in 1911. But the big trouble with that one, and with later models, was that the heat could not be controlled. It wasn't until 1954 that pans with thermostats appeared. Then business boomed: In 1954, 1.1 million electric frying pans were sold; in 1955, 2.66 million, according to trade reports. In this test for heating evenness, five temperature-sensing devices (thermocouples) are connected to a temperature-recording instrument. A laboratory beaker (far left) was used to measure an exact amount of cooking oil, so that the "load" for each pan tested could be kept constant. While the distribution of heat varied somewhat across the cooking surfaces of all 18 pans tested, it was judged sufficiently even for any cooking on all except 1 model.

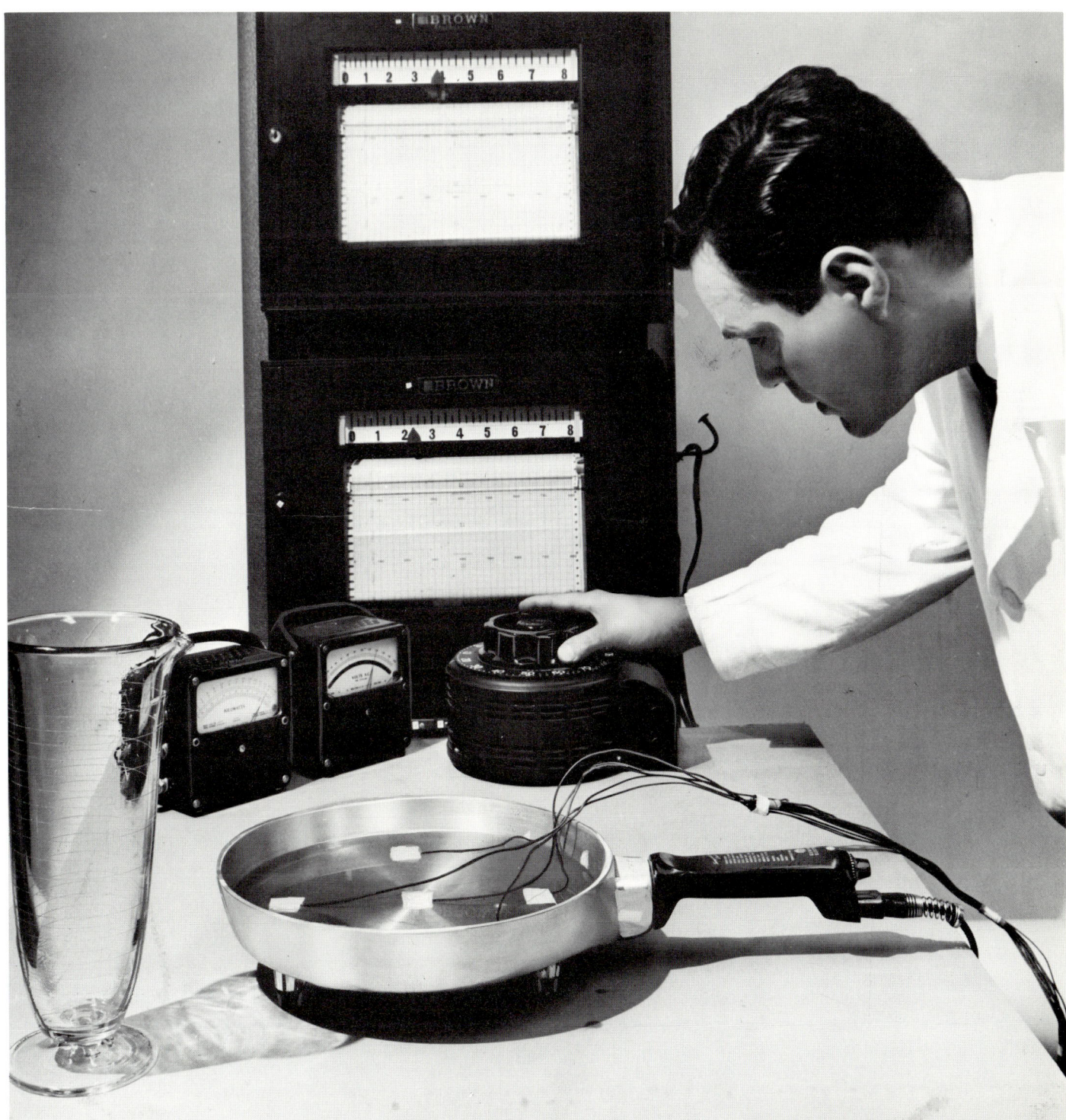

Power
Mowers

Power lawn mower sales increased thirtyfold in the ten years preceding this report—from about 100,000 units to more than 3 million. CU's report covered 42 gasoline-powered mowers—25 hand-propelled rotaries, 5 self-propelled rotaries, 11 reels, and 1 hammer-knife model. No test apparatus can judge grass-cutting ability, convenience, or maneuverability. Teams of horticulturists, agricultural engineers, mechanics, laborers, and students did the testing in late winter and early spring on acres of lawn (some grown especially for this purpose) on the grounds of two southern universities. The tests were designed to evaluate each mower's cutting ability (on grasses of various types and densities and on tall weeds), maneuverability, handling and adjustment ease, and, in the case of self-propelled models, traction. After performance and convenience tests, the mowers were run for 20 hours, then retested. Rotaries were found to be hazardous, but more versatile than the reels.

A Transistor Pocket Radio

OCTOBER 1957

In its first report on small-sized portable transistor radios (May 1956), CU hopefully looked forward to a downward trend in cost and an upward trend in quality in these gadgets. For that report, the $75.00 seven-transistor Zenith Royal "500" was top-rated. Here (on table in foreground), the Emerson 888 ($44.00 to $48.00, depending on color) was found to compare favorably, at a significantly lower price. Widely advertised as "the world's only eight-transistor tubeless pocket radio," the Emerson was tested for a number of electrical characteristics in CU's "screen room," a room completely enclosed in copper screening (ceiling, floor, and walls) to shield the test product from all radio-frequency signals except those generated for testing purposes inside the room. Although the Emerson 888 was found to perform quite well, neither it nor the Zenith performed as well as portable radios with vacuum tubes. (CU knew of no other pocket radio that had more than seven transistors; but in transistors, as in vacuum tubes, numbers alone do not determine performance.) The small-sized, transistorized Rockland Rambler 1-S and 1-S-R battery-operated phonograph and radio-phonograph in the background at right were judged to have poor sound quality, but their convenience, CU felt, compensated for their shortcomings and they were rated Acceptable nevertheless.

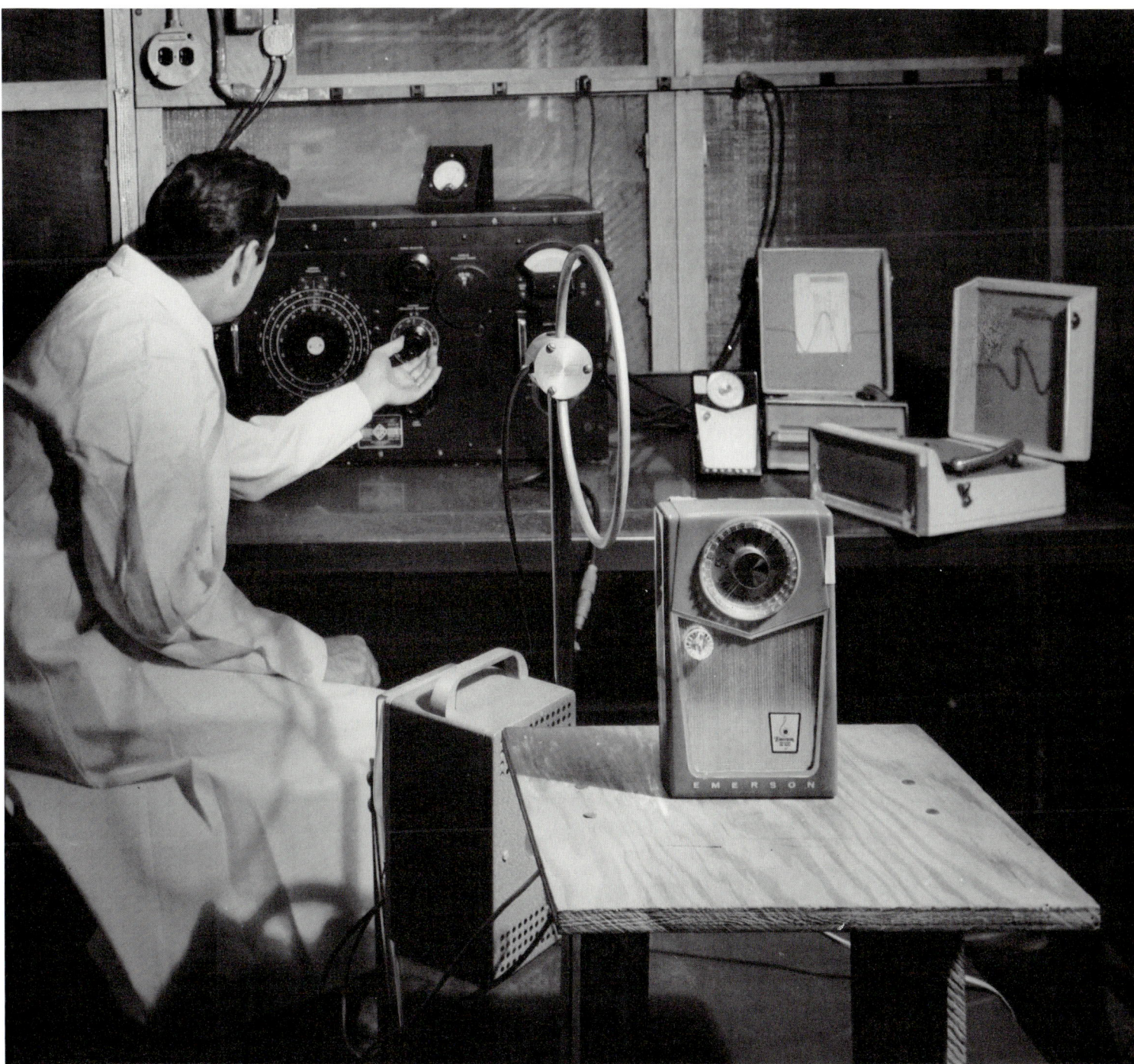

Coffee Makers

CU's tests of 21 coffee makers covered 18 percolators and 3 vacuum-type models, most of 8- to 10-cup capacity. The majority were finished in gleaming chrome plate or stainless steel and cost from $16.88 (plus shipping), for a Sears percolator, to $39.95, for a Cory vacuum-type. Vacuum-type coffee makers have an upper and lower bowl separated by a filter. Water is boiled in the lower bowl. Steam pressure from the boiling water forces it into the open-topped upper section, from which the water is drawn back into the lower container by gravity and by the slight vacuum created by cooling steam. On its way down, the water passes through ground coffee and is filtered. In the Cory vacuum-type model tested, it took some force to assemble the top and bottom bowls. However, if too much pressure was applied too quickly, a miniature water geyser resulted.

Work-Counter Surfaces

MARCH 1958

Linoleum was king of the countertops until after World War II, when newer materials—rigid plastic laminates (Formica), flexible plastic laminates, calendered vinyls, and printed vinyls—began to appear. CU's 1958 tests were aimed at evaluating the durability and ease of maintenance of these relatively new and popular materials, and at comparing them not only with linoleum, but with wood, stainless steel, and ceramic tile. In this test for stain resistance, technicians applied 33 substances to each counter surface, including lemon juice, vinegar, beet juice, grape juice, ink, coffee, tea, mustard, shoe polish, iodine, ammonia, laundry detergent, and drain cleaner. The rigid plastic laminates, flexible plastic laminates, and ceramic tile did best, while stainless steel and wood ranked Poor in this respect, stainless because it stained severely with some common materials and wood because it was stained by a wide range of household materials.

Barring cost as a consideration, CU found ceramic tile and the rigid plastic laminates to be the top performers overall.

Hand Lotions and Creams

MARCH 1958

Accoring to CU, a good hand lotion or cream "can smooth, soothe, and help make supple a skin made rough from house-cleaning chores; exposure to cold, dry weather; or excessive use of soaps and detergents (dishpan hands)." CU purchased at least 3 samples each of 28 brands of lotion and 11 of cream and submitted them to subjective as well as objective tests. Expert cosmetic consultants participated in use tests and evaluated coded, unidentified samples. Acidity and alkalinity measurements were made in the laboratory, where products were also tested for uniformity, consistency, emulsion type and quality, and shelf stability. To rate the products' stability when not in use, each lotion and cream stood at room temperature in capped test tubes for two months. Chemists examined samples for odor changes and microscopic deterioration in physical states. On both counts, most brands were judged satisfactory.

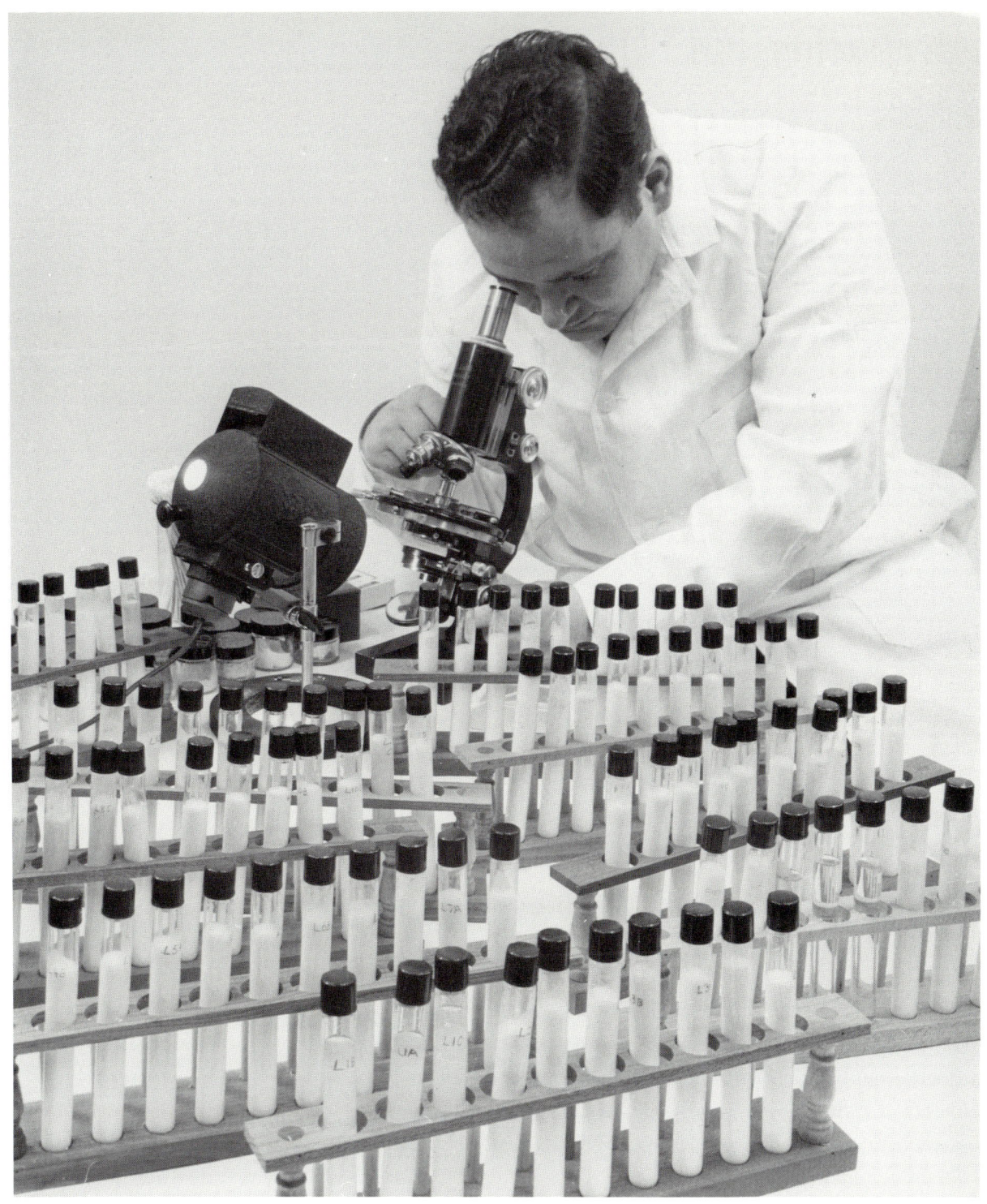

High-Fidelity FM Tuners

MARCH 1958

CU upgraded its test facilities in 1958 to better assess the sound quality of hi-fi components, and to better control the test conditions. Here a technician builds a new piece of laboratory test equipment—a distortion analyzer—to supplement listening tests for FM tuners and other high-fidelity equipment. CU designed listening tests to be as objective as possible. Off-the-air tests were eschewed in order to eliminate variables that could affect judgments significantly—frequently poor-quality FM signals of the time and FM program material content.

Automobile Tires

MAY 1958

Rayon- and nylon-cord, tube and tubeless tires were subjected to eight 400-mile test runs, held at 60 miles per hour by drivers experienced in road-test methods. After each run, the tires were weighed to determine how much rubber had worn away. At the end of 3,200 miles, an abrading machine removed the remaining tread. The weight of the rubber removed was then used to calculate tread life. After removing the tread, CU tested blowout potential by submitting each tire to a plunger test for carcass toughness. (All blowouts are a result of a rupture in the tire carcass; the tougher the carcass, the greater the protection against this potentially dangerous mishap.) To calculate the energy required to rupture the carcass, a hydraulic press was used to force a 1¼-inch steel rod with a rounded end through the inflated tire carcass. Several such determinations were made at various points on each tire. Without exception, the nylon-cord tires proved to be considerably tougher than any of the rayon tires.

Lawn Sprinklers

JULY 1958

CU tested 23 sprinklers—ranging from a very simple rotating device priced at $1.39, to two elaborate oscillating machines priced at $47.50 and $55.00—measuring how fast, far, and evenly they distributed water. Empty cans, placed at one-yard intervals in this grid pattern for oscillators, and in a radiating pattern for rotating models, caught the sprinkled water, and by measuring the amount in each can, CU's engineers were able to judge the uniformity of distribution and to determine the size of the area effectively sprinkled by each model. The oscillators as a group proved disappointingly nonuniform in water distribution. Two rotating models, the Allenco Parkside ($6.50) and the Sunbeam Rain King Automatic K-2A ($9.95), were top-rated and judged Very Good. Uniformity of distribution was considered the most important requirement for scoring high in the Ratings. Tests were conducted indoors so that wind would not affect the results.

High-Fidelity Loudspeakers

DECEMBER 1958

Affordable high-fidelity loudspeakers were just coming into their own at the time of this report. CU selected 27 models out of the 500 or so then on the market, based on practical limitations of price and physical size. In one of several laboratory tests, CU used a specially calibrated microphone (on the left) to "listen" to each loudspeaker in an echo-free room, in which virtually all sound was absorbed by the walls, floor, and ceiling. The microphone measured such factors as frequency response, total sound output at high frequencies, transient distortion due to resonances, and other types of distortion. The heavily insulated room was used so that only the sound radiating from the loudspeaker would be measured. Along with the laboratory tests, each speaker was also submitted to controlled listening tests in CU's sound room. CU concluded that it wasn't necessary to spend $1,000 or to buy a speaker the size of a boxcar to obtain that deep bass and those pure highs. One of the best speaker systems tested, in fact, was also one of the lowest priced—the Acoustic Research AR-2 (13½ × 24 × 11 inches), a Best Buy at $89.00 in an unfinished birch cabinet. The other top-rated models included two KLH speakers ($209 and $119) and another Acoustic Research model ($172).

Automobiles—1959
Chevrolet Bel Air V-8/Six

FEBRUARY–JULY 1959

Though CU recorded about 40 different dimensions on each car it tested in 1959, nearly all of these measurements required evaluation to give them meaning. For example, the trunk of this 1959 Chevy sedan was plenty large—with luggage capacity big enough for four two-suiters and seven weekend cases—but form interfered with function. The sheet metal "wings" at the rear of the trunk formed a rim that ranged in height from 12 inches at the center to 19 inches on the sides. It took quite an effort to lift a heavy piece of luggage into the trunk, because everything placed inside—or taken out—had to be lifted over that barrier.

Photographic Exposure Meters

In any optical test project, controlling light sources is a primary consideration. To measure the accuracy of photographic exposure meters, a calibrated light source was mounted on one end of a lab bench, then placed in a test room whose walls were completely covered in black nonreflective material; the exposure meter was set up in a nonmagnetic holder at the other end. Several shields were placed in between to limit the light to a single path. Meter readings were taken at various distances from the test lamp to determine accuracy at high and low illuminations, and the position of the meter in the holder was varied at each point to determine if it would give consistent readings.

Of the 26 models tested, 5 relatively high-priced dual-purpose meters (which measured both incident and reflected light) were top-rated. The only other top-rated model was a reflected-light-only meter that was one of the most accurate tested, and, compared with meters that ranged up to $34.50 list, was indeed a Best Buy at $6.25.

Automatic Dishwashers

DECEMBER 1959

CU technicians prepared to test automatic dishwashers for washing ability by applying more than 20 different foods—including egg yolk, cooked cereals, heavy stew, milk, peanut butter, orange juice, and coffee—to dishes, glasses, and flatware. Lipstick stains were applied to some cups, glasses, forks, and spoons; cigarette ashes were added on some items. After standing for a period, the dishes were readied for washing by removing as much of the food as gravity and three swipes of a knife-blade could dislodge and stacking them as might be done normally at a table or sink. The still heavily soiled dishes were then loaded into the washers and allowed to stand overnight before being washed. Five dishwashing detergents were used in a statistical design that made it possible to evaluate the relative washing ability of the detergents themselves, as well as the dishwashers, and to permit comparisons of machines and detergents in combination. Cleanliness of the washed dishes, glasses, and flatware was judged based on sight and touch. Two top-rated Whirlpool models (FU-70 and FP-50) washed all but a relatively few pieces of CU's heavily soiled dishes to a radiant sparkle. They did almost as well when the soiled dishes were left to stand for a full twenty-four hours instead of overnight. And, when CU's engineers gradually reduced the quantity of detergent used, these machines with no detergent at all produced cleaner dishes than some models did with the help of a detergent.

Other factors considered in dishwasher performance included drying ability, loading convenience, controls and flexibility, varying capacities, differences in rack design, and operating cost.

Dishwasher
Detergents

DECEMBER 1959

Fewer than a
dozen brands of detergents special-
ly tailored for dishwashers were on the market
in 1959. In conjunction with its dishwasher project
that year, CU tested five of them—Dishwasher All, Cas-
cade, Calgonite, Finish, and Electrasol. When it came to washing ability, no significant differences among the five could be dem-
onstrated. In a test of corrosive action, however, differences did
show up. The chemicals in some detergents attacked dinnerware decorations called "overglaze" patterns, which are often found on fine china,
and particularly on antique dinnerware. Since over-glaze patterns sit
atop the dish glaze, it is usually possible to distinguish them from under-
glaze and in-glaze decorations by running a finger over the surface of the
dish, or by holding the dish up and looking at it by reflected light. An
over-glaze pattern will be raised and will reflect the light quite differ-
ently from the rest of the dish. In this test, a dish with over-glaze
decoration was cut into eight segments. The four segments of
the upper half were placed in a hot detergent solution for
zero, two, four, and six hours (left to right). The pattern's
progressively severe fading is evident. The four
segments on the bottom, immersed in a
different detergent, hardly
suffered at all.

Automobile Seat Belts

FEBRUARY 1960

By 1956, substantial evidence—much of it based on pioneering studies conducted at Cornell Aeronautical Laboratories—indicated that auto seat belts could markedly reduce injuries in accidents by restraining car occupants in their seats, preventing them from being thrown bodily around the car or hurled out onto the road or pavement. At the time of this test, four years later, the car equipped with seat belts was still something of an oddity. In fact, by estimation fewer than 1 percent of American drivers used seat belts in 1960. CU's shoppers, surveying the seat belt market in four major cities, had difficulty locating test samples for this report. In metropolitan New York City, nearly half the automotive supply stores canvassed did not even stock seat belts.

CU installed each sample belt in this test car and buckled it around a metal framework "pelvis" form. Here, a technician is shown activating a hydraulic device that applied a measured force to the metal pelvis (5,000 pounds for 3 seconds in this particular test). Only 9 of the 43 brands tested were judged acceptably safe.

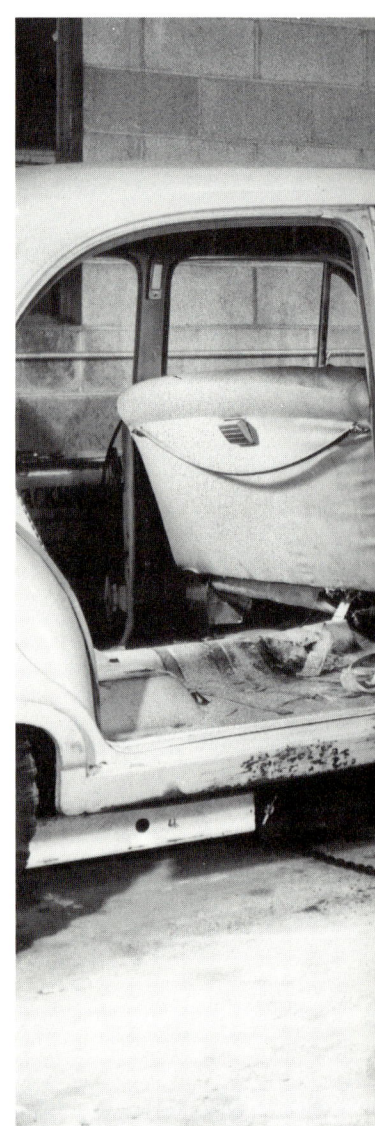

"Minor Brand" 21-Inch Black-and-White Television Consoles

MARCH 1960

Letters asking for information about "minor brand" TV receivers prompted CU to test eight console models—A-M-C, Andrea, Muntz, Olympic, Setchell-Carlson, Supre-Macy, Trav-ler, and Truetone, all of which had limited distribution. Consumers seem to perceive these "private label" or "custom brands" as having virtues that mass production could never create. Here the minor brand sets are lined up for a laboratory check with the test pattern from CU's closed-circuit TV transmitter. The test pattern permitted evaluating each set's ability to reproduce detail, and any tendency to blur or distort images. After conducting its standard series of laboratory tests and engineering evaluations, CU concluded that anyone expecting special qualities in these minor brands would face serious disappointment. "Not only are the sets here essentially the same as the 'name' brands," CU wrote, "but the 'minor' television brands are, in many instances, apt to cost the buyer more for equivalent quality."

Electric Hair Dryers

MAY 1961

A commercial hair dryer served as a standard for comparison with portable hood-style electric models. Temperature-sensing thermocouples in the subject's hair were wired to the temperature recorder at right. Measured temperatures were then correlated with the subject's reports on comfort. General Electric, which was top-rated, turned out to be the most capable of the home hair dryers tested. It came equipped with a flexible hose, a hood with superior air-diffusing abilities (minimizing complaints about too much heat), a more effective blower, and a stable base. The GE did not match the commercial model's drying speed; the commercial machine proved to be about 30 to 40 percent faster. But, by contrast, the slowest of all the hood-type dryers tested took about three times as long as the GE.

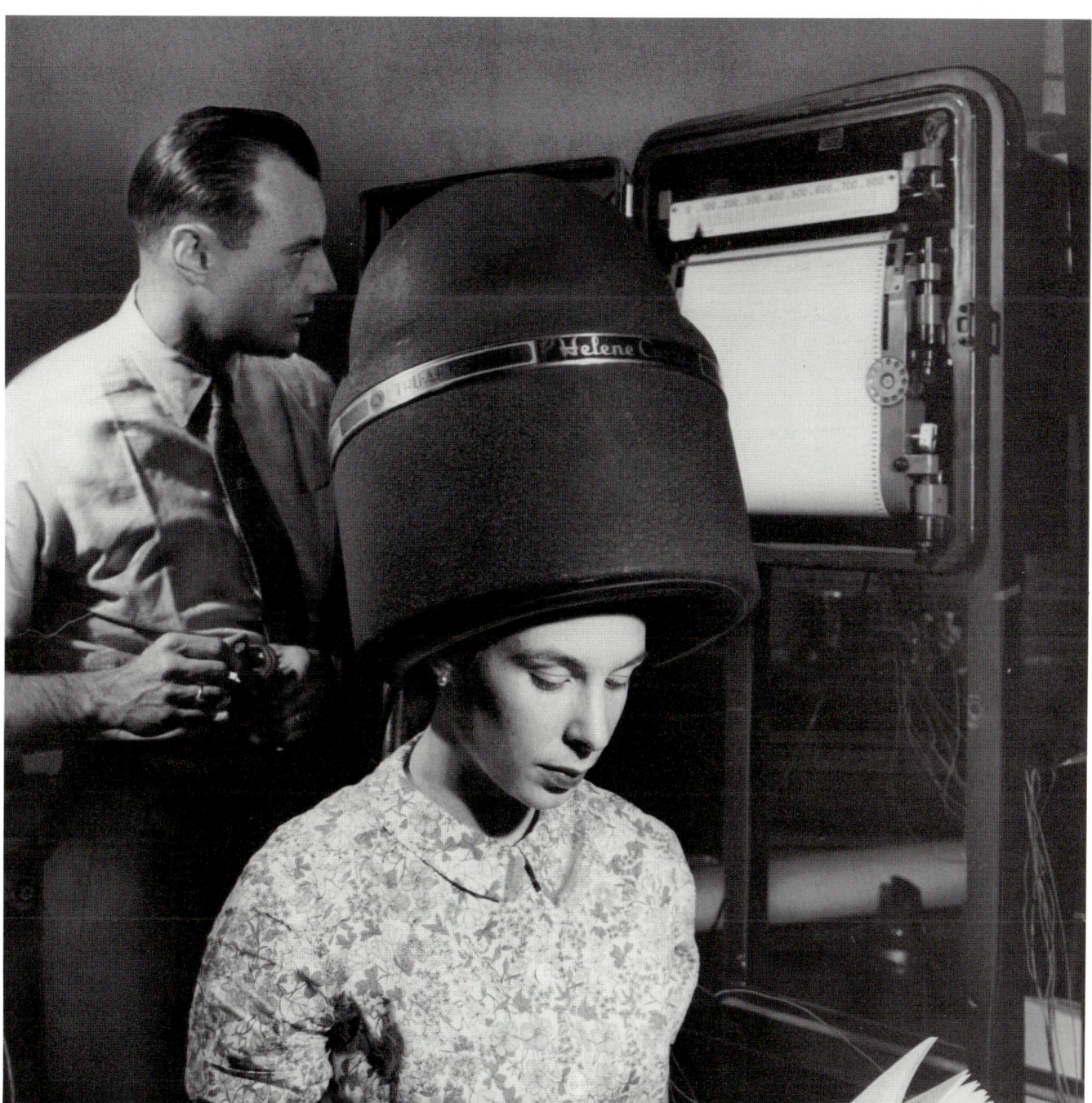

Children's Knit Briefs

SEPTEMBER 1961

Six samples each of 27 boys' models and 25 girls' models of underpants were tested; all test samples were size 12. This temperature and humidity controlled chamber ensured that the test findings were consistent from day to day, since physical properties of textile materials can vary with temperature and humidity. At left, a technician assesses undergarment fit on standard-sized dummies, making sure that after nine launderings the briefs adjusted readily to the waistline without strain in the crotch and leg openings. CU's tension test (center) showed that when new, after nine launderings, and after heat-treatment to simulate aging of rubberized materials, the waistbands in most models maintained the proper amount of elasticity necessary to hold the briefs comfortably on the body and allowed for further stretching without undue effort. At right, a technician weighs a sample on an analytical balance. Both top-rated models—Carters Model 6449-507 ($.89) for girls and Boyville Cat. No. 1131 (2 for $1.78) for boys—were considered relatively high-priced.

Gaylord the Pup

Like all basset hounds, Gaylord, a mechanical toy dog, got around rather gracelessly on stumpy legs. Gaylord, in fact, had to push pretty hard to go a short distance. Here, an engineer is "walking" Gaylord on a wire leash connected to a milliammeter measuring the dog's appetite for batteries. "It should not be too optimistic," CU wrote, "to hope that a $10 toy will hold together (and also hold a child's attention) for at least six months. During that period, some parents may need to replace Gaylord's batteries every week, at a cost more than his original price."

The test was prompted by a letter from a *Consumer Reports* reader who observed: "Children don't understand money and it's a very hard thing to try to explain why we can't put batteries in Gaylord every time they want to play with him."

Room Air Conditioners #1

JUNE 1963

CU engineers created a controlled temperature and humidity environment to test room air conditioner performance. The test setup consisted of a chamber divided in two by a heavily insulated wall. Here, a technician installs an air conditioner in a windowlike opening in the wall. The part of the chamber on the other side of the wall, the part containing the "outside" portion of the air conditioner, was heated to simulate hot, muggy midsummer weather conditions, with temperatures ranging up to 115°F. The technician is working in the "indoor" half of the test chamber, inside a "room" about the size of a bedroom. The maze of temperature-sensing themocouple wiring that surrounds him helped determine how well the unit cooled the inside room. Room heaters, humidifiers, and fans helped to maintain predetermined test conditions within the inside room. Even with no furniture in the room and with the air conditioner mounted in an optimum location, the test models differed perceptibly in their ability to distribute air evenly without drafts or relatively warm or cool areas detracting from comfort.

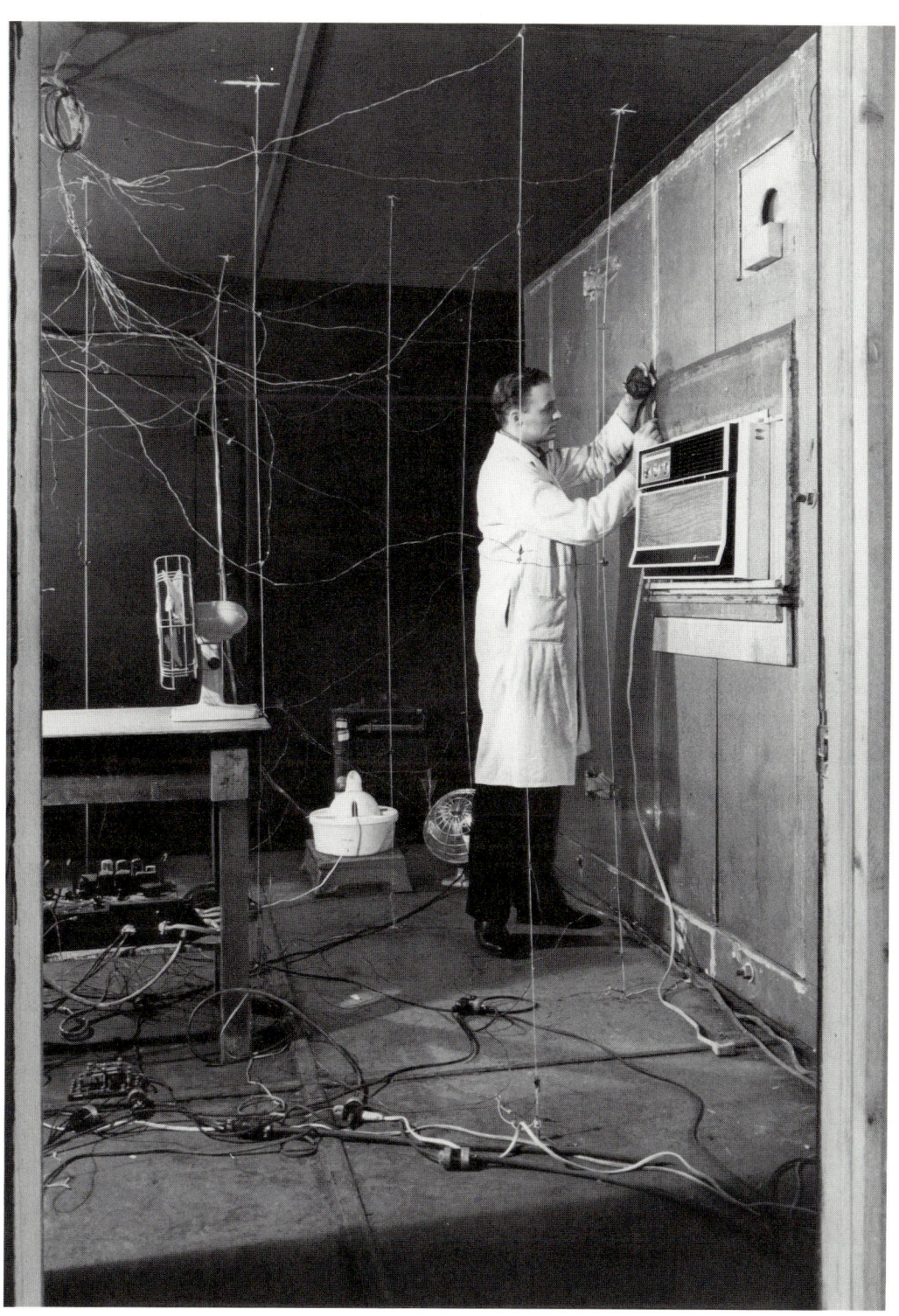

Room Air Conditioners #2

JUNE 1963

A technician monitors instruments outside the controlled temperature and humidity test chamber used to check the performance of room air conditioners. The instruments reveal conditions inside the room and measure the air conditioners' electricity usage.

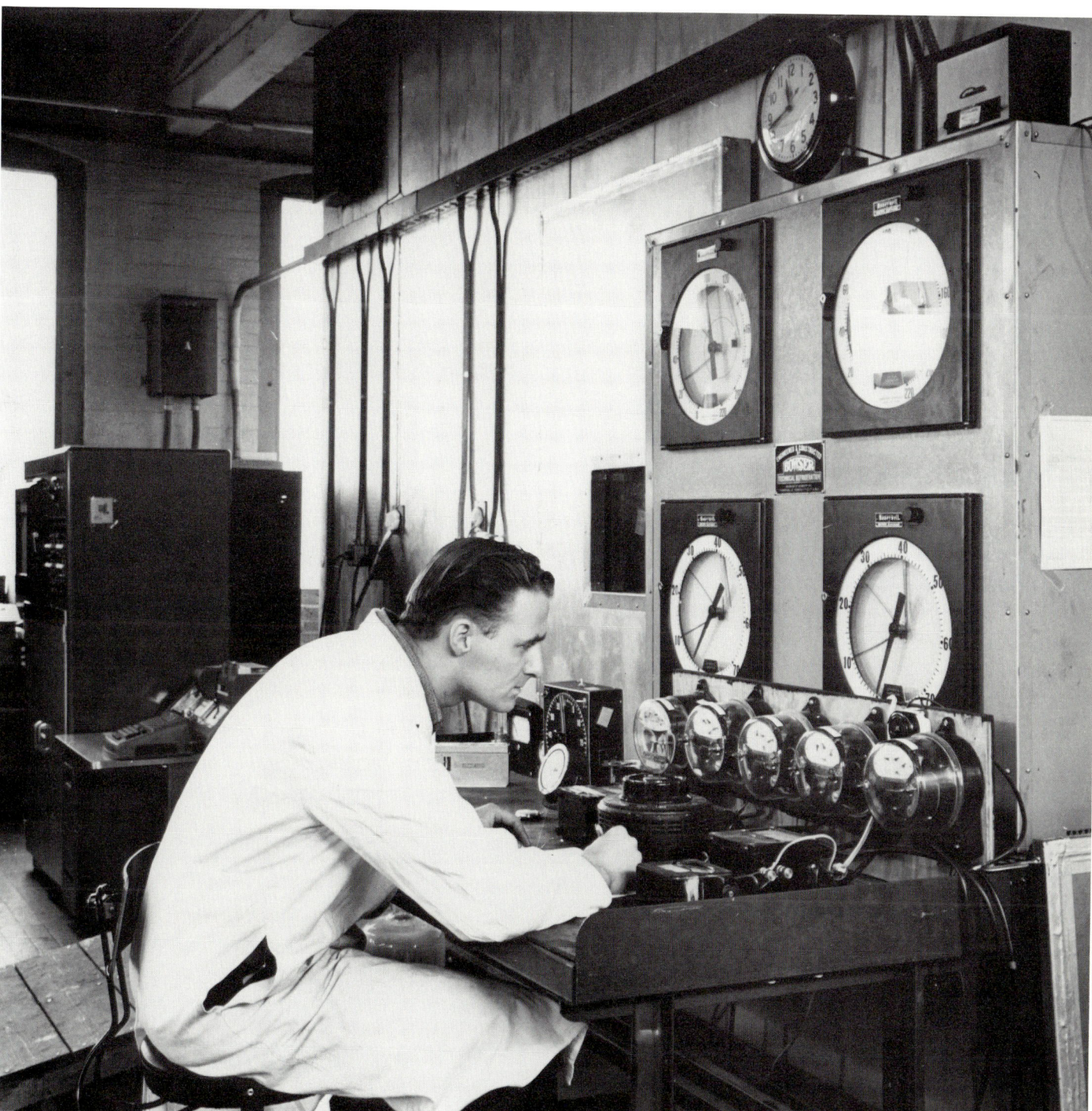

Automobile Safety Restraints for Children

JUNE 1963

In mid-1962, before automobile safety seats and mandatory child safety-seat laws existed, CU bought and tested all the children's restraining devices its shoppers could find—a total of twelve. CU conducted the tests at the Swedish Government's National Institute for Materials Testing in Stockholm. A specially designed dummy approximately 42 inches tall and weighing 44 pounds, about the size of a five-year-old child, was strapped into a seat on the dynamic-test cart, which was repeatedly crashed against a fixed concrete and steel barrier. The effects were observed by high-speed photography.

Of the nine devices still on the market at the time CU published its report, none could be considered Acceptable without some qualification. According to CU, the Rose Safe-Hi Auto Safety Belt No. 890 (pictured here) offered maximum protection. It consisted of a combination chest and lap strap secured to a floor-anchored strap that passed vertically around the seat back; a crotch strap kept the lap strap on the child's hips. Two other devices, a vest-type harness and a "tot cushion" that had to be used with an adult seat belt, which had to be purchased separately, gave only fair protection but were rated Acceptable nevertheless.

AM/FM Portable Radios

AUGUST 1965

An open field provided realistic environmental conditions for AM/FM portable radio tests. To determine a set's sensitivity, or ability to bring in weak stations, a radio-frequency signal generator (foreground) sent a test signal to the sets (not pictured) via the antenna at left. Signal strength, measured at the sets' loudspeaker terminals, gave an indication of each radio's relative ability to pick up the test signals. "Sensitivity and selectivity should be considered together," CU advised. "The former refers to the set's ability to bring in a weak signal, the latter to its ability to discriminate between stations that are close together on the dial. A set with high sensitivity needs good selectivity, too."

Light Bulbs

AUGUST 1965

CU tested five major brands of bulbs, measuring their light output with this integrating (or Ulbricht) sphere apparatus (foreground). Specially formulated, high-reflectance white paint coated the sphere's interior. A new bulb, suspended in the exact center of the sphere, was lit with a precisely regulated current. A sensitive photoelectric cell and meter measured the light output, in lumens, when the bulb was brand new and again after it had burned for 500 hours. None of the brands quite came up to manufacturers' claims.

The light socket rack (background), regulated to a constant 120 volts, tracked lamp life. Some bulbs burned out far short of their rated life; others well exceeded their expectancy. But most samples lasted just about as long as their manufacturers advertised they would—750 hours.

Portable Electric Heaters

OCTOBER 1965

A network of 50 temperature-sensing thermocouples, rigged up in CU's controlled temperature and humidity test chamber, determined each model's ability to heat the "living zone" (up to 5 feet above the floor). In order to improve the thermocouples' temperature-sensing properties, engineers placed them inside blackened spheres—fashioned out of toilet-tank floats. Thermocouples attached to small squares in the living zone registered the heaters' performance at "spot heating" small areas (30 inches wide by 5 feet high) 3 feet in front of the unit, where someone might sit or stand to be warmed quickly.

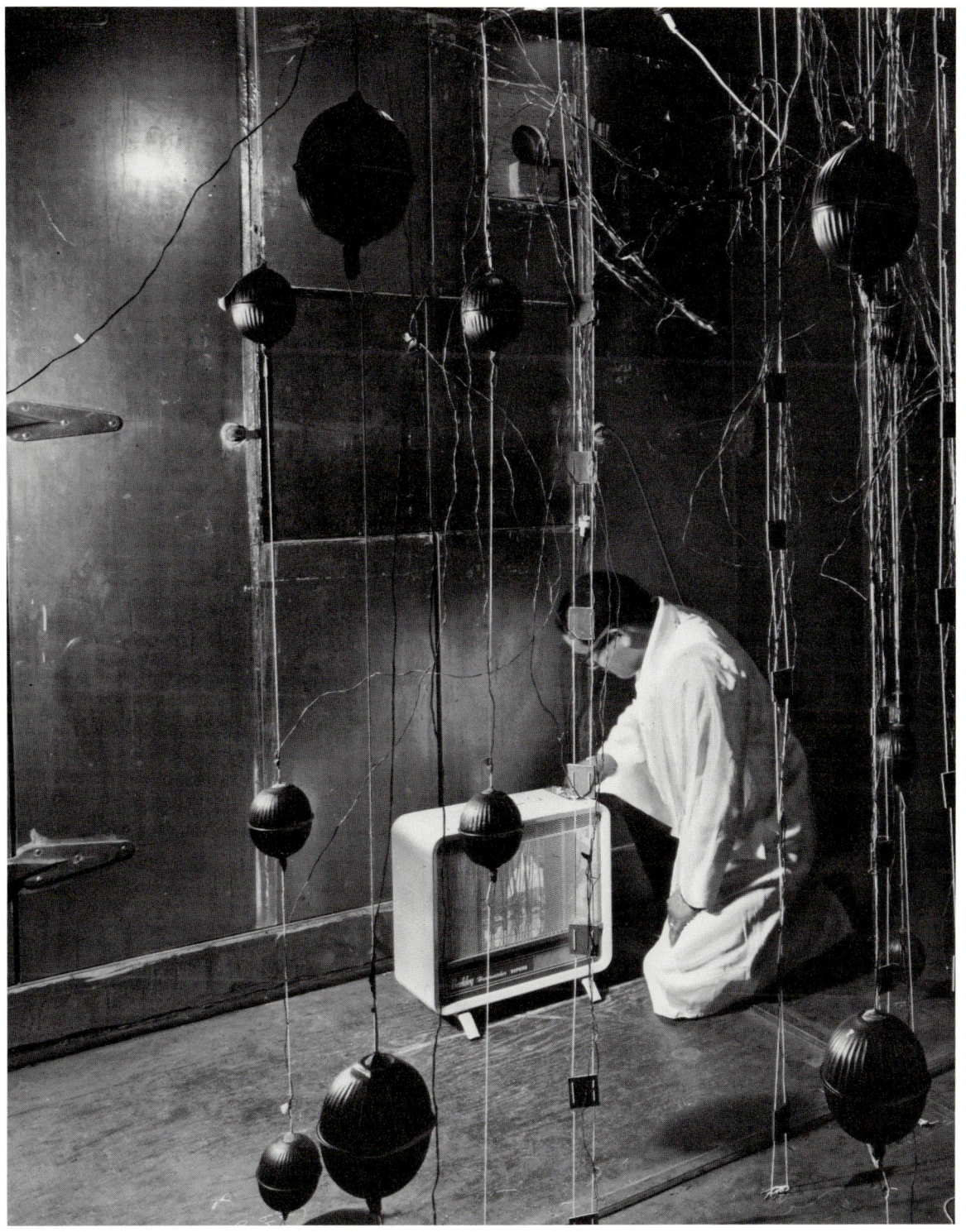

Linoleum and Roto Vinyl Floor Coverings

FEBRUARY 1967

C U tested linoleum and rotogravure vinyl as alternatives to the more expensive, more elegant, and more durable vinyl plastic floor coverings. A woman wearing the spike-heeled shoes common to the era exerted a pressure of about one ton per square inch on a floor. In an indentation-resistance test, flooring samples were mechanically subjected to loads as high as 2,040 pounds per square inch for 10 minutes. Resulting dents were measured immediately, 1 hour later, and 24 hours later. The linoleum samples recovered very well; little indentation remained after 24 hours. Some roto vinyls, however, did not recover quite so well.

Flammable Hair Rollers

MARCH 1968

"While I was boiling my Q.H.S. Hair Rollers, I was distracted by a phone in another part of the house. After about 15 minutes my children called out, 'Your hair curlers are on fire!' I had expected a little sizzling flame and was bowled over to see a jet of flame actually hitting the ceiling."

So began a letter from a *Consumer Reports* reader in Connecticut, prompting CU to test Q.H.S. curlers and two other brands of very similar design—New Solo Quick Set Rollers and Bacarola Minute Set Rollers. All three were essentially small plastic cylinders partially filled with paraffin wax. The user heated the cylinders in boiling water until the unseen wax melted, wrapped her tresses around them, and locked the hair in place with a meshlike plastic shield. However, if she inadvertently let the water boil away, the cylinders soon melted, releasing paraffin that continued to heat until it suddenly ignited. Attempts to put out the fire with water resulted in a geyser of flame as shown in the photograph.

CU's report led the Federal Trade Commission to ask manufacturers to include the following caution on labels: "Warning: Fire may result from allowing water to boil away. In event of fire, DO NOT EXTINGUISH WITH WATER: an explosion will result." The FTC also requested that the labels advise using baking soda on such fires or smothering the fires with a lid or a frying pan.

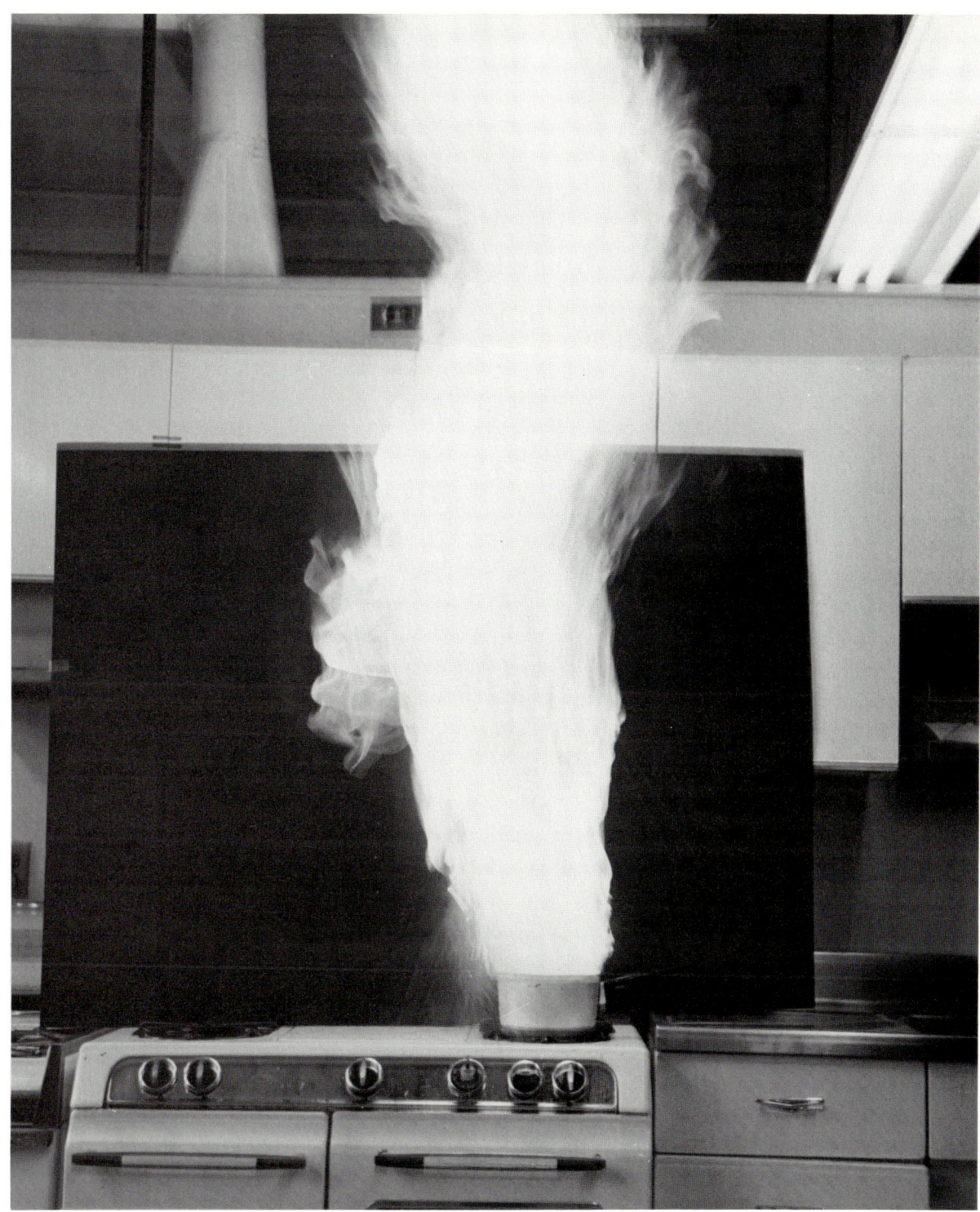

Automobile Tires

AUGUST 1968

CU testers measured tire rupture resistance by driving tire samples over a protruding steel pin at 60 mph. The pin's height was gradually raised with successive runs until it ruptured the tire. Two tire samples for each brand were used—one slightly broken in, the other bald.

Differences in performance were significant. The steel-belted radial tires—even the bald samples—held up until the pin height was more than 4 inches. The others, on average, failed at pin heights of 3¼ inches with full tread and at less than 3 inches when bald. In the other major performance categories—stopping distance, traction, and tread life—results did not relate as clearly to tire type, although radial-ply tires showed high-quality performance more often than not.

Antifouling Boat Paints

APRIL 1969

Fouling is the term boatowners use to refer to the tenacious plant and animal organisms that accumulate below a boat's waterline. No hull material in common use—wood, glass fiber, aluminum, plastic, steel, or concrete—is immune to fouling. In salt water, hard-shelled fouling—such as limpets, snails, mussels, clams, and barnacles—can slow the passage of the speediest vessel. Freshwater fouling is less formidable; still, freshwater boatowners must reckon with grasses and algae. Painting hull surfaces below the waterline with a good antifouling paint can give effective protection against fouling organisms. All antifoulants contain a chemical poison that dissolves in minute quantities around the hull and repels or kills fouling organisms. CU tested 30 different formulations. To measure the paints' resistance to marine fouling—the chief Ratings criterion—aluminum, wood, and glass-fiber test panels were suspended from a floating dock in high-fouling seawater near Miami for eight months and inspected monthly. A second set of test panels, also submerged, went through alternating periods of rotation and rest to simulate cruising conditions. Then they were left submerged and at rest for four months to determine the effect of the "cruise" on antifouling performance. Test results showed large differences among the paints. The panel shown here was partially fouled. Other panels were almost completely coated with marine debris, and still others showed hardly any signs of fouling at all.

CONSUMERS UNION.
SERIES NO. 1
29 APRIL 68—7FEB 69
PANEL NO. 3435

Food Waste Disposers

MAY 1970

By 1970, 12.5 million American kitchens were equipped with food waste disposers. CU tested 27 models that year to determine how well they chewed and digested the food they were fed. Each model received a diet of difficult, but not atypical, household food waste: bone scraps (hard), corn husks (tough and fibrous), and citrus rinds (tough, leathery, and bulky). This menu was varied with some less taxing garbage, including lobster bodies, peach and olive pits, banana peels, walnut shells, hunks of potato, and corn cob halves. Technicians also created deliberate "accidents" for the disposers, involving paper napkins, tea bags with strings, paper plates and cups, and plastic knives and forks.

By CU's standards, a good disposer should grind everything fed into it down to a particle size small enough to pass easily through household plumbing. The best that any machine could do in the corn husk test was to reduce the husks to short, threadlike fibers (shown at left). The poorer performing machines discharged more of the longer, coarser fibers (at right).

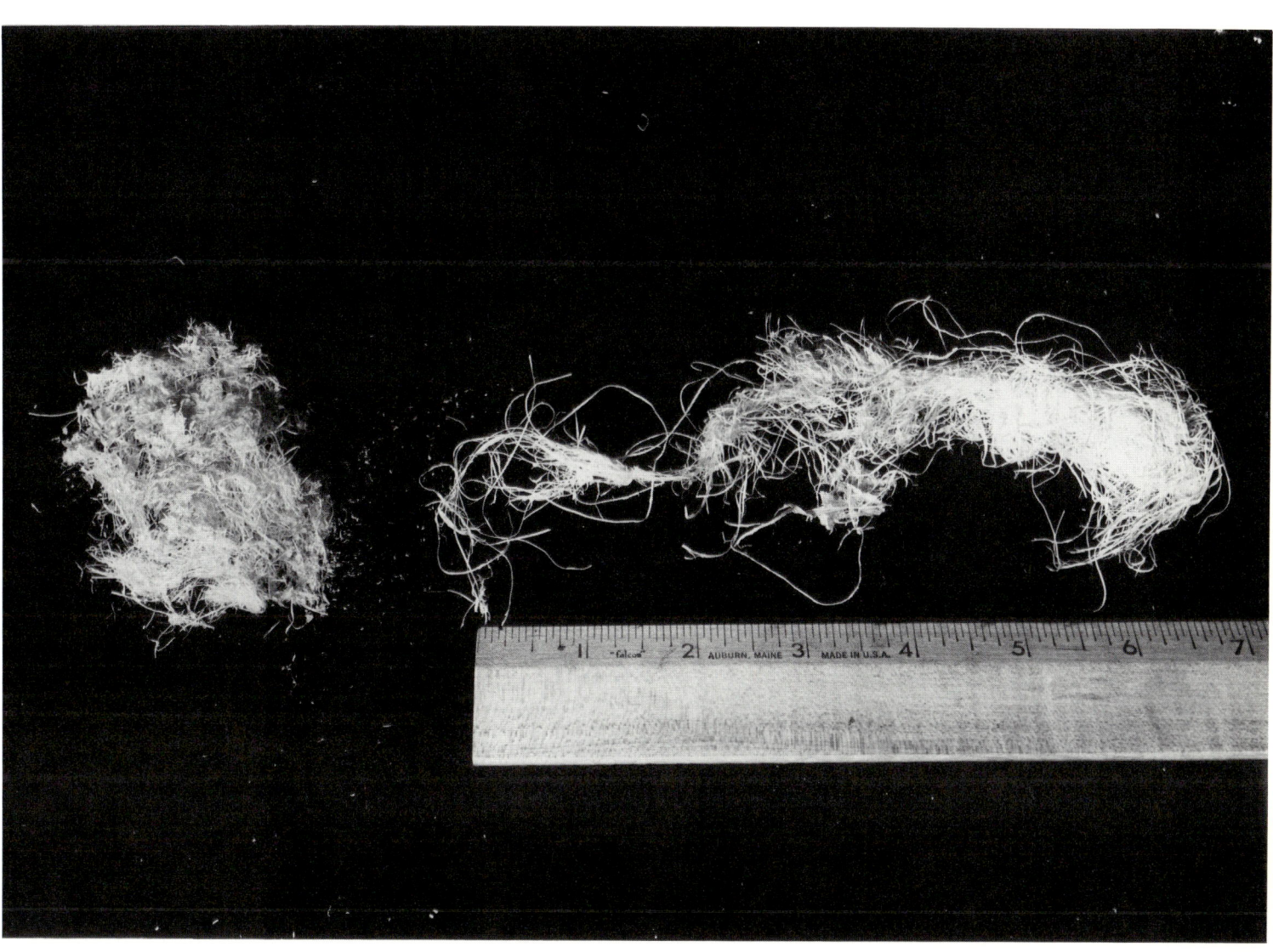

Instant Coffees

JANUARY 1971

A total of 155 consumer panelists made 2,160 taste tests of 45 instant coffees—33 regular and 12 freeze-dried—and rated the coffees on a 7-point scale. Each coffee was made at three strengths—low, medium, and high. Medium strength was derived from the formula recommended as "ideal" for brewed coffee by an organization that represented the governments of 14 South and Central American coffee-growing countries. Low used 30 percent less coffee, high 30 percent more. Three brewed coffees—Maxwell House, Yuban, and Sanka—the largest-selling regular, "premium," and decaffeinated ground coffees, respectively—were also included at the three strengths. With each coffee being judged three ways, and including the 9 brews made from the 3 ground coffees, the panel tasted a total of 144 different beverages, identified only by code number. With a few exceptions, all 144 were liked about equally. Safeway, Chase & Sanborn With Freeze-Dried Flavor, Butter-Nut Freeze Dried Coffee Nuggets, and Stewarts Freeze-Dried were the only four brands preferred over the others frequently enough to be rated Above Average, but only at a specific strength (medium strength in Chase & Sanborn; low strength in the others). Two of the brewed coffees—Maxwell House and Yuban—would also have fallen in the top group had CU rated them, but only at low strength. The test panel did not prefer the freeze-dried instants, on the whole, over the regular instants. But overall, they liked the nondecaffeinated better than the 11 decaffeinated instants.

Binoculars

NOVEMBER 1971

The most important functional consideration in judging binoculars is optical alignment. Because a binocular contains two separate sets of optics—one for each eye—any serious misalignment, either horizontal or vertical, may produce eyestrain or headache.

CU checked binocular alignment on this specially built collimator (the long, cyclindrical device), an optical instrument that generates a light beam composed of essentially parallel rays. Relatively high-priced binoculars fared consistently well in this test. The low-priced binoculars, however, showed significant variations in construction and performance among supposedly identical models.

Zippers

JULY 1972

CU developed a battery of 17 different tests to subject every vulnerable part of a zipper to stress and strain. This tensile strength testing machine registered the force required to tear or separate the chain itself, pull the scoops (teeth) from the chain, or incapacitate the zipper in any other way.

The results? All 26 brands were found to be so consistent in quality that brand distinctions paled to insignificance. Plastic and metal zippers stood up equally well in these punishing tests. And, since price differences among comparable models were negligible, "consumers can consider themselves free to select slide fasteners strictly according to personal needs and tastes."

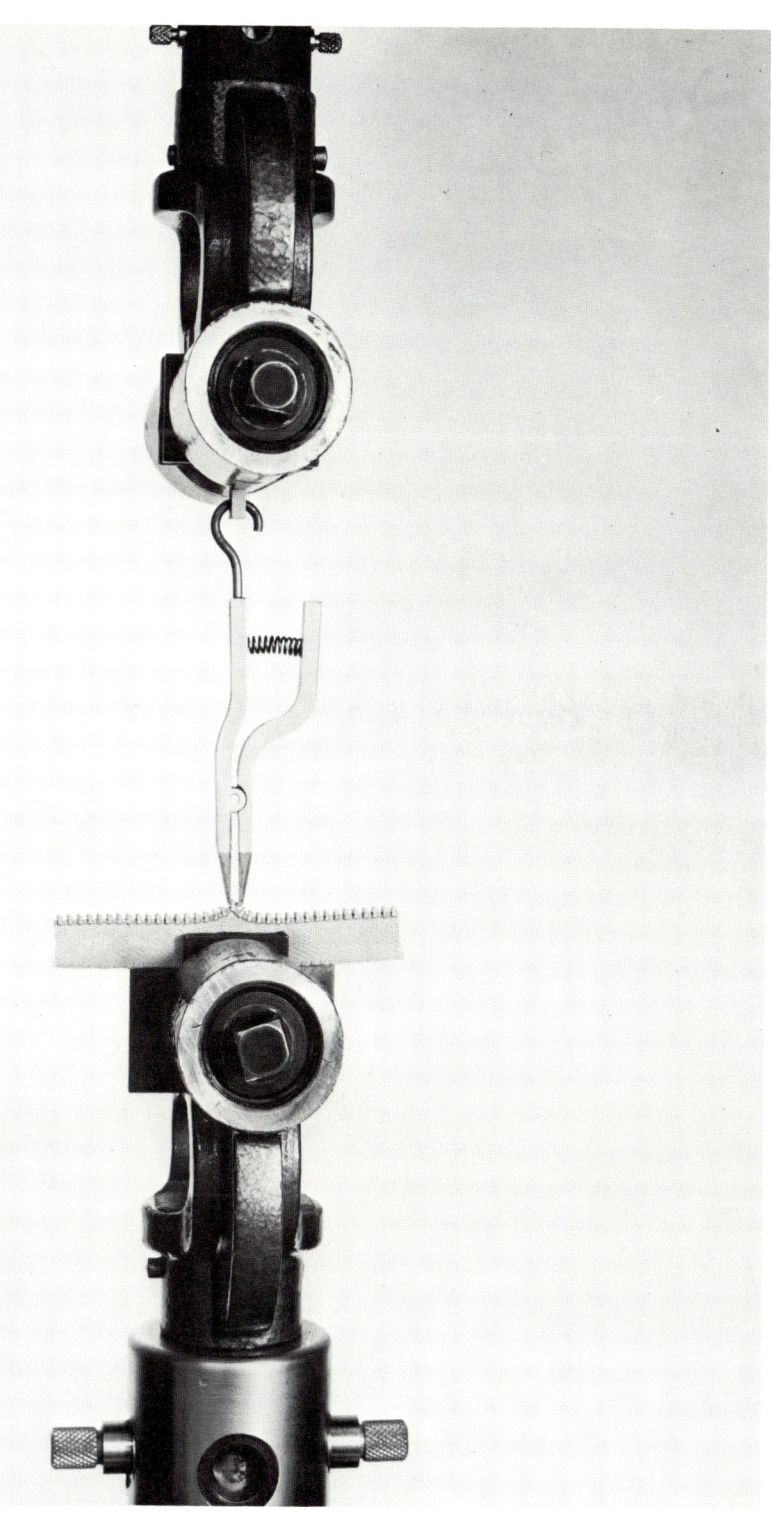

Four-Wheel-Drive Utility Vehicles

SEPTEMBER 1972

The Madison Avenue yarn spinners would have had us believe that the four-wheel-drive vehicles in this test group combined "proven off-road capabilities" with "refined road manners," "toughness and utility" with "comfort and driving ease." The implication seemed to be that these models—the Chevrolet Blazer, International Scout II, AMC Jeep Commando, Ford Bronco, and Toyota Land Cruiser—could serve equally well as recreational vehicles, snow plowers, and family cars. However, none of the vehicles tested proved satisfactory for both on and off the road use, in CU's judgment.

Road (and off-road) tests were done in New England back country, on steep grades, along narrow trails strewn with obstacles, across a shallow stream, and over mudholes—terrain that would be unthinkable for an ordinary passenger car. But on paved roads, the vehicles' handling was uncertain and their rides punishing. And an assortment of safety problems caused CU to rate four of the vehicles Conditionally Acceptable and the fifth Not Acceptable.

"One important factor to consider before buying any off-road vehicle," CU wrote, ". . . is that careless use of such vehicles can destroy vegetation, scar the landscape, and create air and noise pollution. . . . Off-road vehicle enthusiasts should exercise discretion so that they don't destroy delicately balanced wilderness ecologies."

Dinette Sets

SEPTEMBER 1972

CU bought 25 dinette sets for this report, expecting to present its customary type of product story with a list of Ratings. But by the time testing was completed, a different report emerged. First, many of the models had been discontinued by the conclusion of the tests. Second, even though models tested were limited to the intermediate price range—about $100, plus shipping, to $320—the sampling represented only a fraction of the number of models and variations on the market. Third, although differences in design, materials, and construction were noted, CU judged that all the sets—and therefore probably just about any set available in the general price range tested—would be quite durable and would provide the average family with a number of years of good use. Finally, there was the styling, which CU didn't consider.

Here, a tulip base table gets high marks for sturdiness but fails to provide adequate foot space except on the base itself. That raised a problem of marring, particularly because the finish was painted.

Stereo Headphones

An engineer wears headphones fitted with a high-quality laboratory microphone ⅛ inch in diameter and 1½ inches long. With the headphone set in use, this "probe" microphone could be positioned at the entrance of a person's ear canal without disturbing the seating of the headphone. And thanks to its tiny diameter—substantially smaller than the wavelengths of sound encountered in the audible frequency range—the mike could measure sound pressure in the space between the headphone's "speaker" and the ear canal without disturbing the sound field much. Subjects listened to random noise with the probe mike at a fixed distance point near the ear-canal entrance, while a computer automatically processed and printed out the microphone's output. CU based its Ratings in large part on the subjects' frequency response perception in these tests, which included the effects of air leakage around the phones' rims.

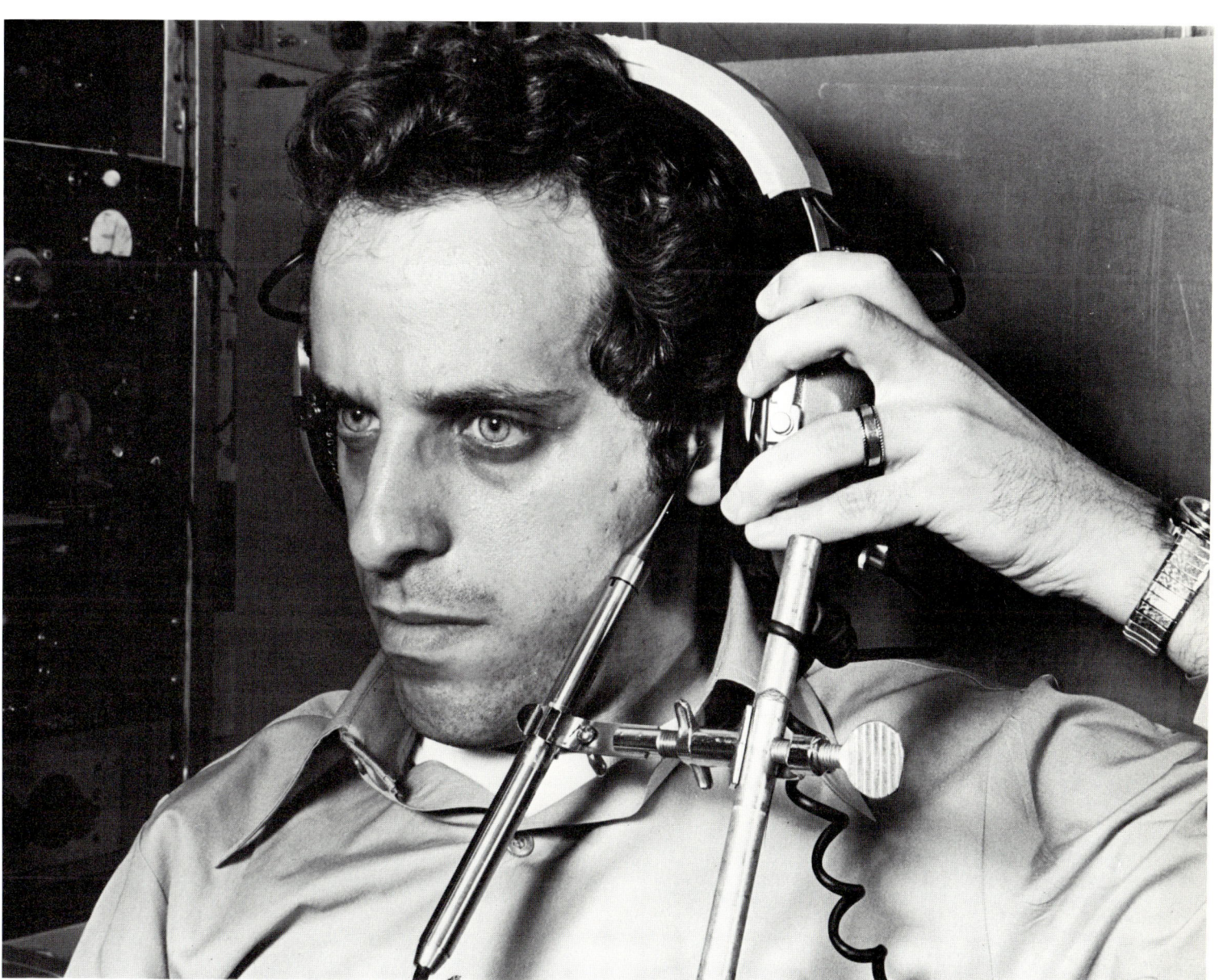

Frozen Fish Fillets

MARCH 1973

Eighteen samples each of 41 brands of frozen perch, sole, cod, haddock, and flounder were examined for the presence of bones in the filleted products. The ruler shown here, along with some of the bones found in the so-called fillets, indicates the size of some of the larger bones. Cod and ocean perch were the most likely to be bony; flounder and sole the least likely. Only 9 brands were judged Excellent or Very Good in quality; 26 were judged Poor or Not Acceptable.

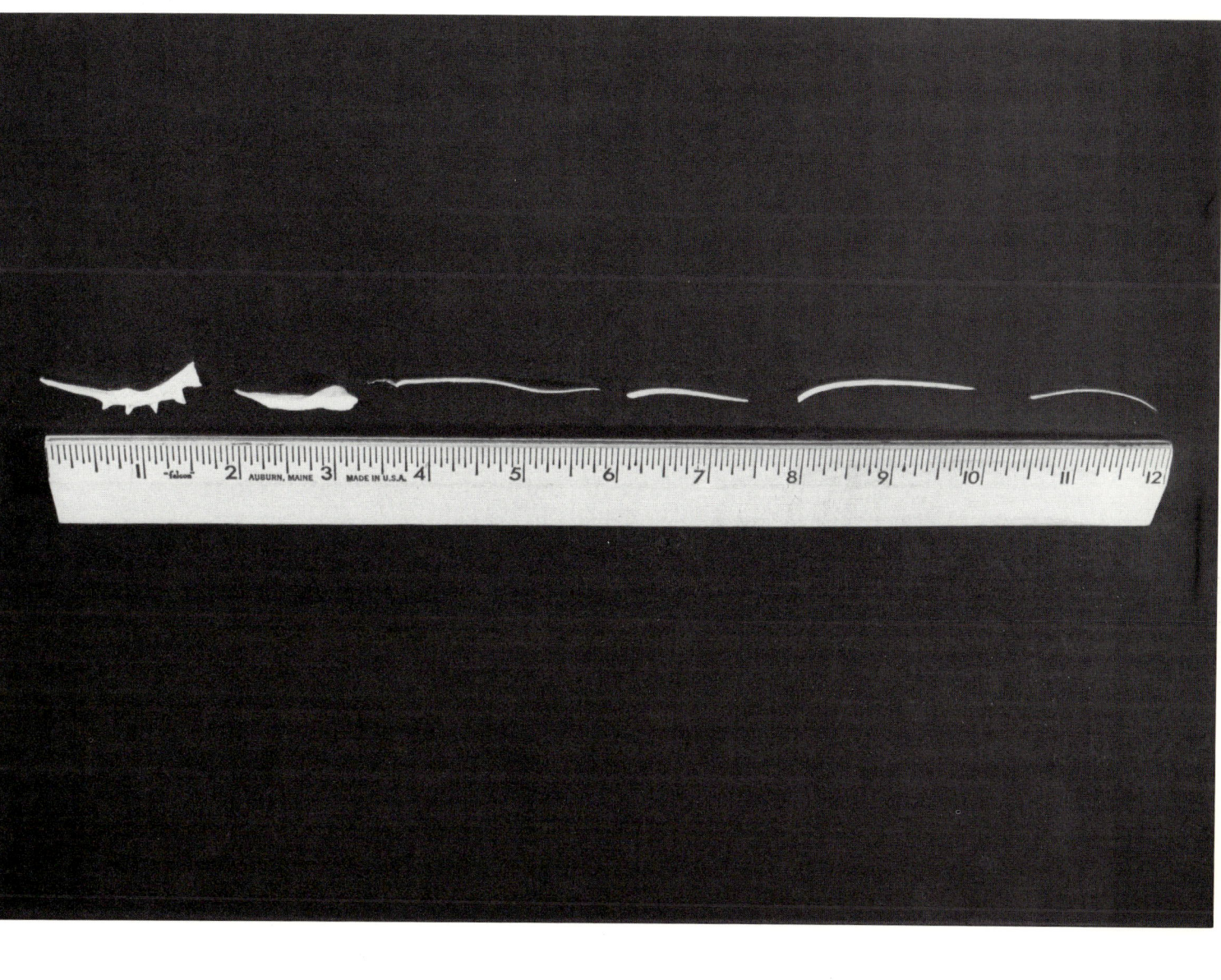

Expensive Loudspeakers

FEBRUARY 1974

By the mid-1970s, acoustic testing at CU had come a long way from the methods used to report on High-Fidelity Loudspeakers in December 1958. Altogether, 20 loudspeakers took their turn in the acoustically neutral environment of CU's anechoic (echo-free) chamber. Each speaker was mounted on a test stand before a battery of precision microphones. Then, a wide-band random noise signal with uniform power in each octave of the audio range was fed into the loudspeaker. The microphones measured sound pressure around the speaker at 10-degree intervals as the speaker rotated by remote control on its horizontal and vertical axes. The readings went directly into a preprogrammed computer that automatically plotted graphs illustrating the speaker's acoustical behavior.

The speakers were then set up in CU's approximation of a home living room, where a panel of trained listeners judged them for sound accuracy and "trueness." In the end: "Much as we admired the quality of our high-priced units," CU wrote, "we don't think the average person would find their quality commensurate with their high prices. Fine speakers, worthy of fine music systems, are available for a good deal less money."

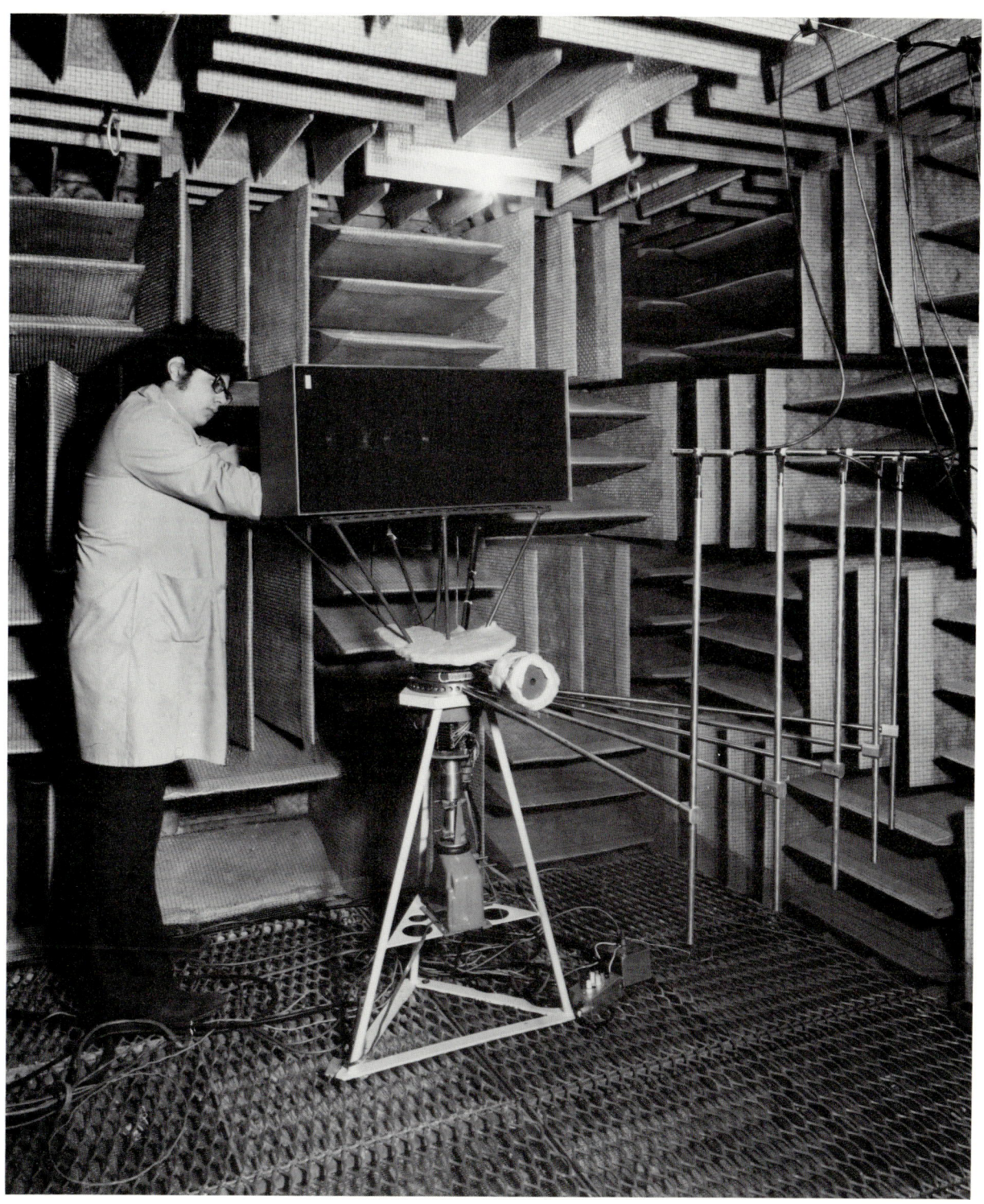

Intermediate Station Wagons

MAY 1974

CU routinely evaluates front-seat comfort and second-seat comfort as part of its automobile testing program, and in the case of the intermediate wagons reported on in this group, third-seat comfort. For the Buick Century Luxus pictured here, comfort in the optional third seat was rated poor to fair for two adults. Climbing into the seat required a long and, for miniskirted women, immodest step. Once inside, a passenger had to stretch to reach and close the liftgate. Furthermore, the seat faced rearward, an arrangement that could make some passengers feel queasy.

Although termed "intermediate," the station wagons tested were about 18 feet long and weighed well over 2 tons. With their third seats in place, the wagons could seat eight adults.

19-Inch Color Television Sets

JANUARY 1975

All 16 models rated for this test had cabinets made partly or wholly of plastic. The kind of plastic used could easily be set burning with an ordinary book match, and would then continue to feed the flames. A TV set deliberately set afire outside CU's laboratory presented this frightening spectacle. The burning cabinet threw off choking fumes and dripped globs of flaming material on the ground. Around the time of the tests, the Consumer Product Safety Commission acted to mandate safety standards for TV sets. Given the fire-starting potential of TV circuitry, TV cabinets henceforth were to be made of material that would act as a fire stop rather than as fuel.

Spot Removers

JUNE 1977

Hundreds of plain white fabric swatches—some made of pure cotton, others of polyester, still others of nylon—are shown air drying in a laboratory area. CU's chemists had stained the fabrics with three particularly nasty mixtures to simulate a spot that might result from eating: a coffee-cream-and-sugar mix, a mustard-mayonnaise-catsup-and-gravy mix, and a mix of several red wines. They also prepared a combination of car grime, grease, soot, and road dust—the kind of stain you might pick up when changing a tire or making another emergency car repair. Technicians uniformly applied staining mixtures to the fabric squares, then administered each spot remover according to its label instructions. Results were compared with those obtained from a five-minute soak and rinse in plain water, and from spotting with a heavy-duty liquid detergent followed by machine-washing in warm water with the detergent.

Only one of the spot removers tested—Whoosh!—consistently outdid the washing regimen. But Whoosh! had to be mixed with water, and couldn't be used, therefore, on articles that couldn't be hand washed. Of 16 brands tested, 4 flunked in CU's eyes for using fluorocarbons as propellants, and 6 others failed for containing a suspected carcinogen or posing excessive fire hazards.

144

Road Emergency Signals

SEPTEMBER 1977

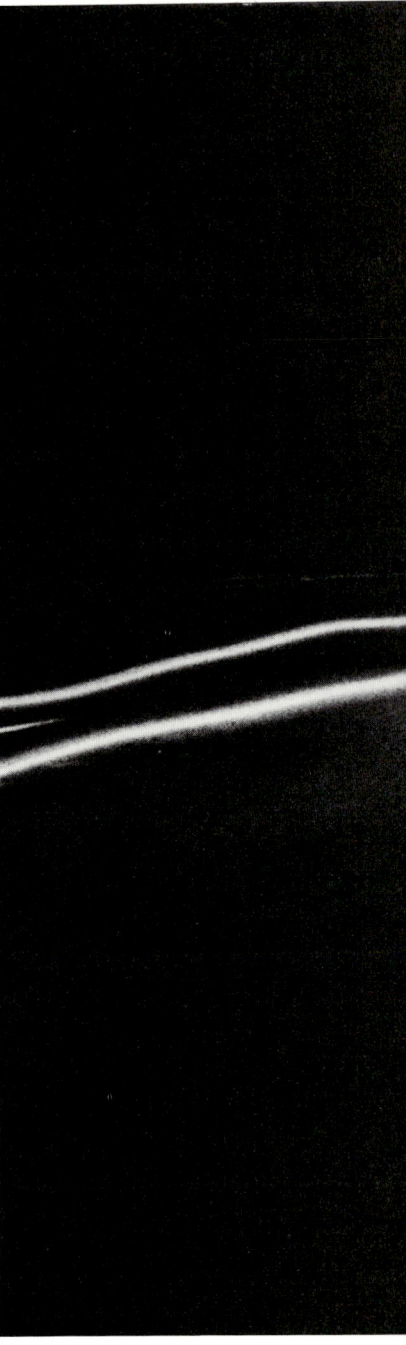

CU simulated the breakdown of a car on a private road to evaluate the effectiveness of three kinds of emergency devices—fusee flares, triangle reflectors, and roof-mounted flashing lights. Effectiveness included not only the visibility of the device from various distances, but also the clarity of the warning message the device conveyed. First, CU tested for meaningful differences in visibility within each type of device. None was detected among the 5 brands of fusee flares or the 11 models of triangle reflectors chosen for the tests, but several brands of roof-mounted lights were decidedly more visible than others. One of the basic goals of the test program, however, was to determine which *type* of warning device was most effective. A representative model flare and triangle reflector were selected for the test, along with one of the more visible roof-light models. The instructions on the triangle reflectors recommended placing one at a distance of 10 feet behind the "disabled" car; a second about 100 feet (roughly 40 paces) behind the car; and a third 200 feet behind the car. CU placed one reflector at each recommended distance but chose its own lane positions—the first (the one nearest to the car), at the traffic side of the lane in which the car was stopped; the second, in the middle of the lane; the third (the one farthest back), at the edge of the lane near the shoulder of the road. The same distances and the same configuration were used to set up three samples of the fusee flares. Triangle reflectors were judged to be the best all-around type of highway warning device. Their high reflectivity, bright orange color, and distinctive shape command immediate attention both day and night, and their ample size helps oncoming drivers judge distances to the disabled car.

Facial Tissues

AUGUST 1978

I t's disconcerting to have a tissue disintegrate in your hand, especially when you're trying to contain an explosive sneeze. That's why "blowout" resistance became one of CU's most important criteria in rating 25 of the most popular brands of facial tissue.

To test blowout, CU engineers devised what has come to be known as "The Great American Sneeze Machine." The test rig consisted of a fixed-position paint sprayer containing air and water; the tissue, held in an embroidery hoop; and a plywood baffle (upper right) with a small oval hole. The baffle was fastened to a pendulum suspended between sprayer and tissue. An engineer squeezed the sprayer trigger, thereby discharging a jet of air and water onto the baffle. Simultaneously, the baffle was released and, swinging in an arc, allowed one fraction-of-a-second spray burst—an explosive, simulated sneeze—to strike the tissue through the hole in the baffle.

To see how closely these laboratory sneezes approximated the real thing, CU recruited staffers (most of whom had colds at the time) for actual use tests. After weeks of sneezing and nose-blowing, test panel judgments generally supported the laboratory findings. Of 25 tissues brands tested, 9 came out Very Good in the sneeze test. Of the others 9 were only Fair, with 7 in-between.

Escape Ladders

OCTOBER 1979

The CU engineer assigned to this project used his own home in a suburban community outside of New York City as the site of these field trials. Ten escape ladders were tested for ease of use and security of handholds and footing.

Almost all of the ladders had a common problem: their designs made little allowance for holding the ladder away from the side of the house. CU found that toeholds were difficult to find and maintain, and in the tests done barefoot, the potential for stubbed toes and other injuries was great.

The model pictured here solved the problem with a set of four short legs attached to each pair of rungs to hold them away from the house. But even this design could not alleviate the difficulty of getting onto the ladder itself. This staffer has just completed a hip roll from a seated legs-out position on the sill and is now fishing for his first foothold on a rung.

Stereo Headphones

OCTOBER 1979

Headphone frequency response can vary widely, depending in part on the size and shape of the head and ears of the wearer. To arrive at an average of those variables, CU used a special dummy, known as Kemar (for Knowles Electronics Manikin for Acoustic Research). Kemar is designed to help engineers predict how things will sound, on average, to real people. Its head and ears have about the same size, shape, and acoustic properties as those of a typical human of medium size.

Here, Kemar stands in CU's anechoic chamber. For the headphone test, however, engineers placed Kemar in CU's listening room. Using a precision microphone in one of its removable ears, they measured and plotted the ear's response to the sound field produced by a pair of high-accuracy loudspeakers. Since the dummy "heard" what a human in that sound field would hear, the engineers could use the response of its ear as a yardstick for measuring the headphones.

The next step was to see how closely each headphone's response resembled the listening room yardstick. The closer it did, the better the headphone. Engineers detached one of Kemar's ears and mounted it on a resilient plate covered with soft plastic foam. The foam was also yielding enough to seat around-the-ear headphones with the tight seal between ear cushion and head that these models generally depend on for good bass response. A strategically placed metal tube helped to simulate the acoustic "leak" caused by human hair and minor irregularities in ear shape. Engineers fitted the ear with each of the tested headphones and measured the phones' response. Finally, a panel of real people listened to music through selected headphones to make sure that subjective judgments squared with objective results. They did.

Automobile Jacks

JUNE 1980

CU tested this inflatable jack as an alternative to the standard-issue jacks found in car trunks for fixing a flat. As the car's engine started, the cylindrical vinyl bladder inflated through a tube from the car's exhaust pipe, and the car raised up by its own exhaust gases. "Rather like picking itself up by its own bootstraps," CU commented. The process took less than 10 seconds. Once the car was raised, a one-way valve kept the bladder from deflating until the user twisted a coupling. Because exhaust gas is poisonous, this jack could only be used outdoors. "The Anser jack does a good job of raising a car with a flat tire," CU concluded. "But we wonder whether it's worth spending $79.00 or more for a novel car jack."

Paper Towels

AUGUST 1980

"The ideal paper towel," according to CU, "absorbs a lot of liquid and stays strong when wet." In one test for wet strength, technicians clamped a towel into an embroidery hoop mounted on a stand, wet it with 10 drops of water, then poured a slow and steady stream of fine lead shot onto the towel. When the towel burst, the technicians stopped pouring and weighed the lead shot. The weaker paper towels held less than a pound of shot. The strongest towels, Job Squad and the single-ply version of Viva, held more than seven pounds of shot, and ranked highest in overall quality out of 30 brands tested.

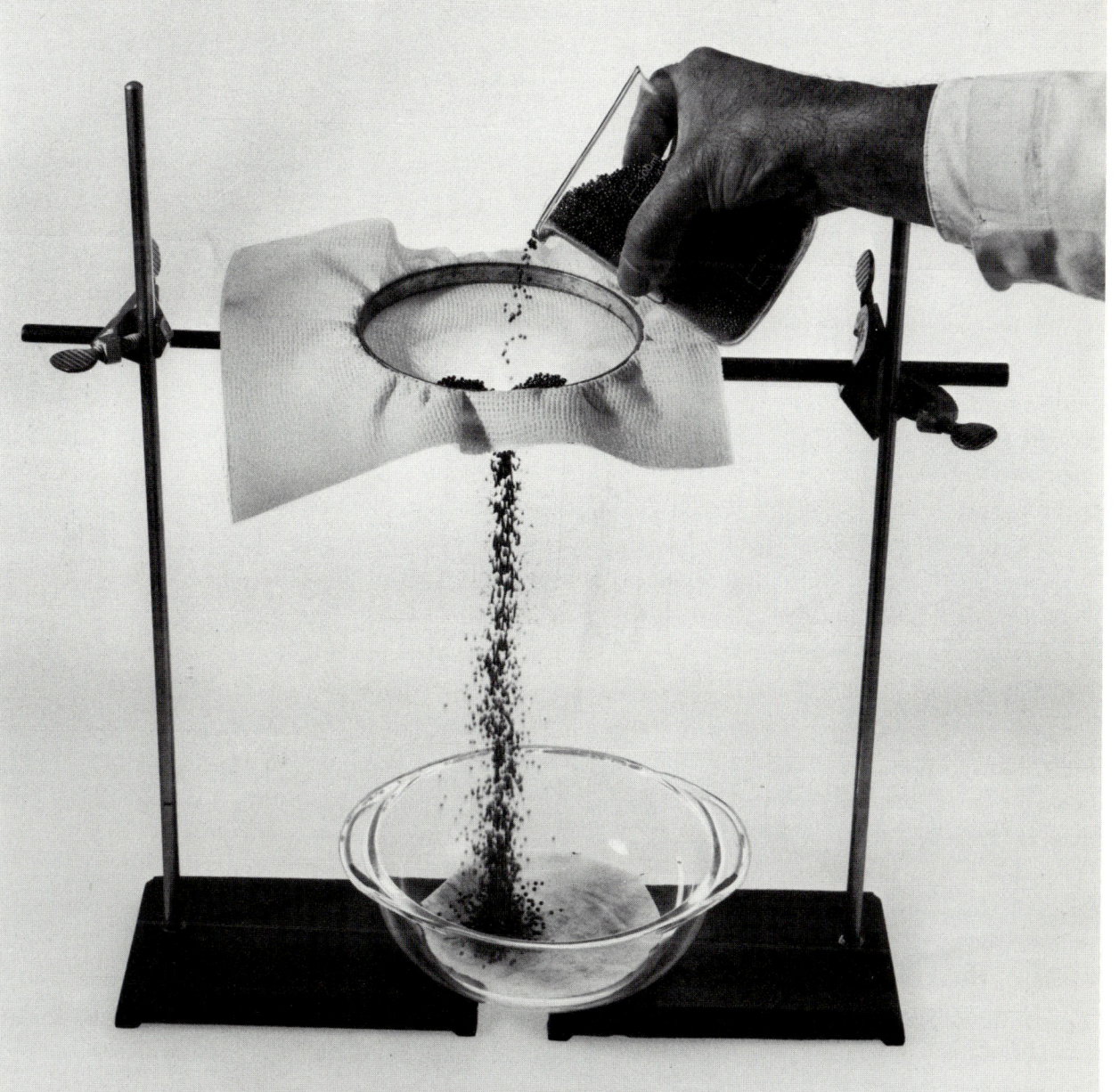

Garbage/Trash Bags

JUNE 1982

The best way to test garbage bags is to fill them with garbage and see whether they break when treated roughly. While CU believes in realistic tests, its engineers drew the line at spending days tossing around coffee grounds and lasagna scraps. Instead, they created some "clean" garbage. For most of the tests, engineers loaded the bags with shiny new tin cans full of dried beans, which they had filled and sealed themselves to a weight of about 18 pounds per cubic foot, the density of refuse used in standard sanitation-industry tests.

During the course of the testing, hundreds of bags—15 samples of each brand and size—were filled, dragged, and dropped. In order to speed the process and make sure every bag was handled in the same way, the engineers devised a contraption they dubbed "Tin Can Alley." The garbage-filled bags were carried along by an overhead conveyor and dropped onto a concrete-topped table, there to break or not. As a special form of torture, the lawn-and-leaf bags were dragged along a nearby concrete "sidewalk" that had been installed over the laboratory floor before being dropped from on high. To test these bags, CU wanted to use a more appropriate debris than tin cans. To get an "outdoor" load, they filled each bag with a 50-pound mixture of pine bark laced with enough gravel to bring the density up to 18 pounds per cubic foot. After the bags were dragged on the indoor sidewalk, they were dropped three times each onto the concrete-topped table. Even with that extremely rough treatment, several brands showed only minor scrapes. A few samples leaked moderate amounts of pine bark and gravel, while most samples of the bottom-rated brands failed.

Peepholes

OCTOBER 1984

"If you don't know or can't identify visitors, don't open the door to them. Instead," CU advised, "screen visitors through an optical viewer, or 'peephole,' in the door."

CU tested a variety of optical viewers—small metal cylinders whose fish-eye lens allows for a wide-angle viewing area—by installing them in a simulated entranceway door in the laboratory. All the viewers worked.

About half the samples claimed to have a viewing angle ranging from 160 to 200 degrees. CU's measurements generally showed those claims to be overstated by 30 to 50 degrees. In no case did a peephole approach 180-degrees of view. Hence, a person pressed flat against the door or an adjacent wall would be outside the viewing angle of any of the models tested.

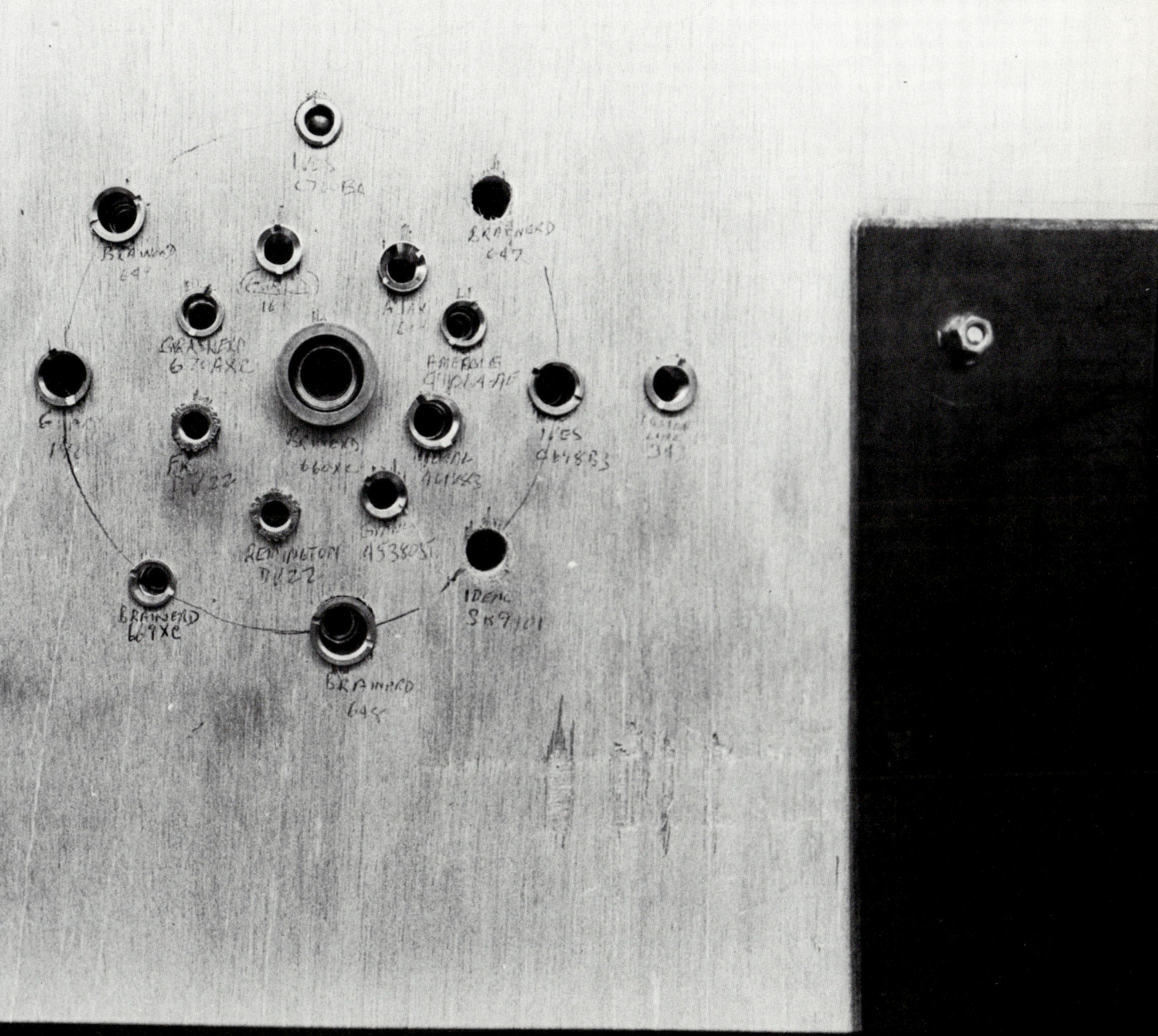

Softsided Luggage

JULY 1985

These mysterious markings represent a portion of the "test track" along which CU panelists pulled wheeled, loaded suitcases much as over-burdened travelers tote their bags around airports. The track, located in the area outside the back door of CU's main building, led up a nearby ramp and included in its course asphalt, a gravel-strewn patch, pitted concrete, and tight curves. The four-wheel bags with narrower wheels were difficult to steer on rough terrain; the bigger (two-inch) wheels on the two-wheelers were easier for many panelists to roll along pebbly surfaces. But all the bags trailed along nicely on smooth straightaways.

Portable Electric Heaters

OCTOBER 1985

C U checked both the performance and safety of 35 electric heaters ranging in price from $35 to $241. In one safety test, CU draped fabric over part of each heater's grille for 30 minutes, to simulate the fire hazard that could occur when a portable heater contacts or comes near curtains or bed linens. Many of the heaters scorched the fabric to varying degrees. But three heaters scorched the fabric and then, within 15 minutes, set it ablaze. These three models were rated Not Acceptable.

Innerspring Mattress Sets

MARCH 1986

Mattresses vary widely in firmness and in the way they conform to the body—both measurable factors. But only individual experimentation can determine how much firmness or conformity anyone may find comfortable or uncomfortable. Beyond that personal judgment, a mattress should retain its original feel for a long time.

CU's mattress "basher," a machine for testing the structural integrity of mattress sets, performed durability tests, designed to show which sets might last longer than others given the same treatment, on twin-size mattresses and foundations. The device, equipped with a buttocks-shaped ram, delivered 100,000 controlled strokes to the center of each mattress set, where a sleeper's weight is concentrated. Then the mattress and foundations were repositioned and the mechanical buttocks delivered 25,000 strokes to the edge, where a person might sit. Upon completion of the test, each set was cut open to assess internal damage. Only 6 of the 32 sets survived the test without any structural damage or significant change in firmness.

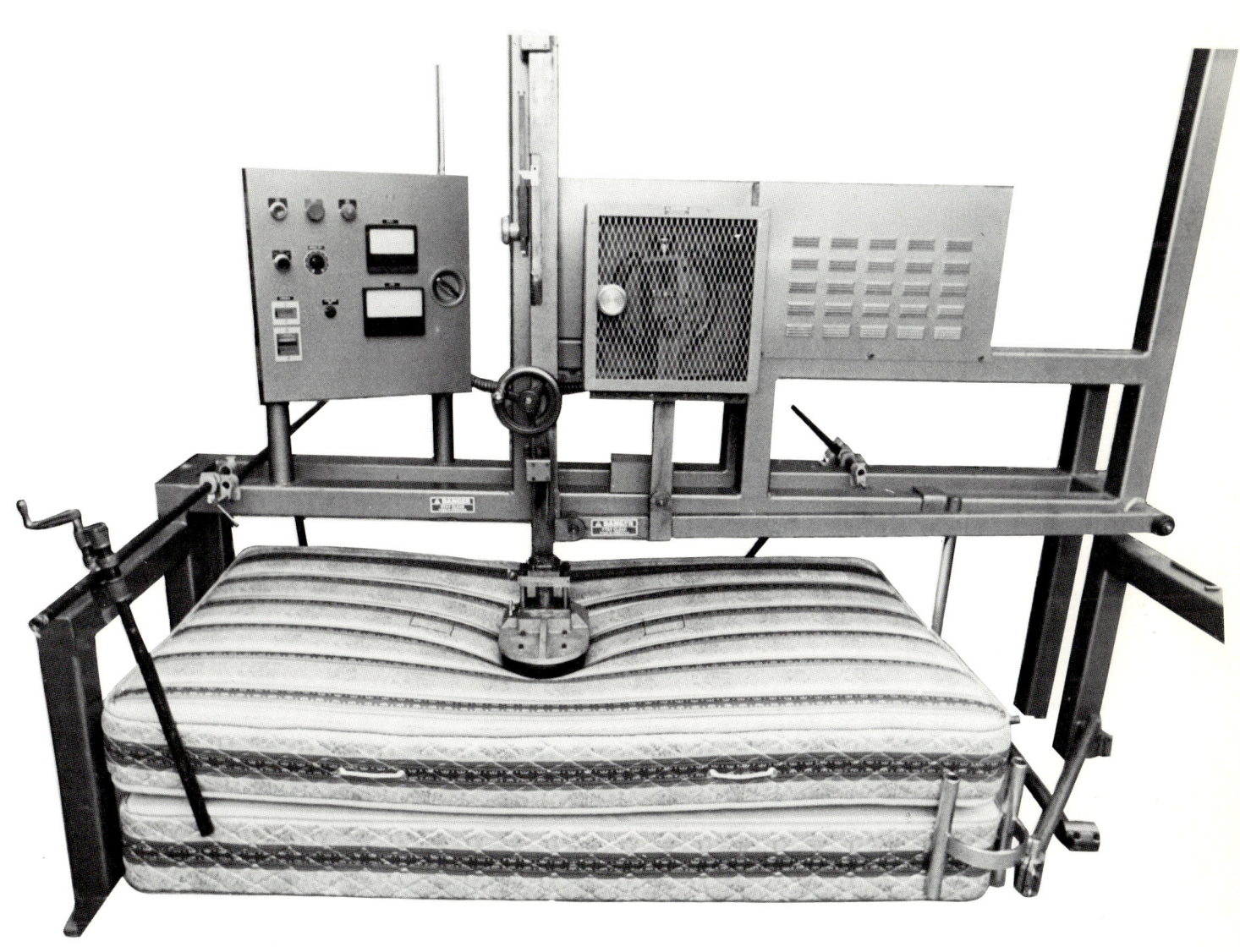